T0055470

Homo Economicus,

the (lost) prophet of modern times

Homo Economicus,

the (lost) prophet of modern times

Daniel Cohen

Translated by Susan Emanuel

polity

First published in French as *Homo Economicus* © Editions Albin Michel,
Paris, 2012

This English edition © Polity Press, 2014

INSTITUT
FRANÇAIS

This book is supported by the Institut français (Royaume-Uni) as part of the
Burgess programme.

Polity Press
65 Bridge Street
Cambridge CB2 1UR, UK

Polity Press
350 Main Street
Malden, MA 02148, USA

ISBN-13: 978-0-7456-8012-5

A catalogue record for this book is available from the British Library.

Typeset in 11 on 14 pt Sabon
by Toppan Best-set Premedia Limited
Printed and bound in Great Britain by T. J. International, Padstow, Cornwall

The publisher has used its best endeavours to ensure that the URLs for external
websites referred to in this book are correct and active at the time of going to
press. However, the publisher has no responsibility for the websites and can
make no guarantee that a site will remain live or that the content is or will
remain appropriate.

Every effort has been made to trace all copyright holders, but if any have been
inadvertently overlooked the publisher will be pleased to include any necessary
credits in any subsequent reprint or edition.

For further information on Polity, visit our website: www.politybooks.com

Contents

Acknowledgements   vi

Introduction   1

1 Gross Domestic Happiness   5

2 Work: A Diminishing Value   20

3 The Decline of Empire   34

4 De-Centring the World   54

5 The Great Western Crisis   76

6 Darwin's Nightmare   91

7 The Postmodern Condition   106

Conclusion   124

Notes   127
Index   145

Acknowledgements

I thank Francis Wolff for his friendly and profound reading of this manuscript, and I thank my editors Richard Ducousset and Alexandre Wickham for their prophetic advice.

How often have I watched and longed to imitate

when I should be free to live as I chose,

a rower who has shipped his oars,

and lay flat on his back in the bottom of his boat,

letting it drift with the current,

seeing nothing but the sky gliding slowly by above him,

his face aglow with a foretaste of happiness and peace.

Marcel Proust, *Swann's Way*

Introduction

Everybody is looking for happiness – 'even the person who is going to hang himself', as Pascal said. The modern world can almost be defined by the idea that happiness on earth is the goal of humankind. On the scale of centuries, that outcome seems to be materializing. According to Thomas Hobbes, yesterday life was 'nasty, brutish and short'. Today, at least in the rich countries, it is long and prosperous; wars and epidemics are retreating, while democracy and freedom of thought now reign.

But that is not how people reason. For most, the harshness of life does not seem much reduced compared to how it was yesterday. About 14 per cent of Americans under the age of thirty-five have experienced a major episode of depression. In France over the last thirty years, the consumption of anti-depressants has increased three-fold, and suicide attempts among the 15 to 25-year age bracket have doubled. In the United States, indicators of wellbeing dropped by almost 30 per cent compared to the levels attained in the 1950s. In study after study, the result is the same: happiness regresses or stagnates in rich societies, in France as elsewhere.

How can we understand the paradox of a society that gives itself a goal it always fails to achieve? One answer comes immediately to mind: humans cannot be happy because they can get used to any improvement. Whatever the progress that has been made, of any kind, it quickly becomes ordinary. The page is always blank for any happiness yet to be constructed. But since humans do not manage to foresee this adaptation, their dreams of happiness remain inexhaustible. This is not in itself discouraging, since this trait is also the one that enables humans to keep an intact faith in a better future, a form of eternal youth. But this trait invites us to understand its mechanics. In this inexhaustible quest, what are the specific characteristics belonging to the contemporary world? Why does happiness seem harder to attain today than yesterday, despite (in the rich countries) much higher material wealth?

An anecdote will help us to grasp what is in play. The director of a blood bank wanted to increase his stock, so he came up with the idea of offering a financial reward to blood donors. To his amazement, the result was exactly the opposite: the number of blood donors fell. The reason is not very mysterious. People who give blood are showing generosity; they are driven by moral behaviour, a concern for others. The act of paying them changes everything. If it is no longer a matter of helping others but of earning money, their participation changes in nature. A different sphere of their brain is being called upon. The moral person leaves the room when Homo Economicus enters. Each of the two certainly has a role, but they cannot be seated at the same table.

To reach his goal, the director of the blood bank in fact had only two options: either he should give up his new arrangement and try to go back to the previous situation, or he should forge ahead by increasing the bonus to motivate donors to come forward anyway. For the last thirty years, much of the contemporary world has chosen the second of these alternatives. To function under the sole aegis of Homo Economicus, it has increased the rewards and the punishments. To keep its promises, it consequently creates a more unequal world.

This anecdote is drawn from a book with the fitting title of *Les Stratégies absurdes (Absurd Strategies)* by Maya Beauvallet. She shows that businesses have turned their management strategies upside down. By increasing bonuses, sometimes sharpening rivalry among their own employees, corporations are acting like the director of the blood bank. They are making the moral value of work disappear: any concern to do well, any search for one's colleagues' approval. Thus one major international corporation boasts that each year it eliminates 10 per cent of its staff in order to maintain the remaining employees' taste for winning.

And the economy is not the only thing affected. The mania for ranking things (schools, hospitals, researchers, friends on Facebook) is omnipresent. The best wins out over the good. The two most painful moments in adult life, according to all studies, are being fired and getting divorced. They have both become more frequent. In the case of marriage, I want to be able to leave my partner if I no longer love that person. But since this inclination is reciprocal, couples are becoming more precarious. To use a term from a leading light of economic analysis, Gary Becker of the University of Chicago, the labour market and the 'matrimonial market' now obey the same logic: to maximize the profit of the encounter, until new opportunities appear . . . Some win, others lose, but in every case the equilibrium becomes more fragile. A neo-Darwinian world in which the weakest are eliminated and subject to the contempt of the victors is everywhere taking hold.

Darwin himself, however, warned against the social uses of his theories. The 'struggle for existence' is a metaphor that he thought should be used carefully. As the biologist

Jean-Claude Ameisen has shown in a poetic book,[1] Darwin insisted on the existence 'in many animal species; including humankind, of phenomena of cooperation among individuals of the same species, which he called sociability and sympathy'. But the modern world has gone in the opposite direction, to privilege competition over cooperation.

How can we understand this evolution? The list of possible causes is long. The fall of the Berlin Wall, the stunning rise of financial capitalism, globalization, and the information society are among the most frequently cited causes. Other sociological explanations had been advanced, such as the attitude of baby-boomers towards parental authority. The central paradox of this era, however, is the following: The economy is summoned to take charge of the direction of the world at a time when social needs are migrating towards sectors that are hard to place within the scope of market logic. Health, education, scientific research, and the world of the Internet form the heart of postindustrial society. None of these belong to the traditional economic mould. While human creativity is higher than ever, Homo Economicus imposes himself like a sad prophet, a killjoy of the new age.

At a time when billions of 'new arrivals' are coming to the table of a vacillating Western world, it is urgent to rethink from top to bottom the relation between individual happiness and the forward march of societies. By avoiding the two symmetric dogmatisms – knowing better than the people what is good for them, or inversely, letting them cope on their own – the question that is posed is nothing less than that of the course of the world society that is being constructed before our eyes.

1

Gross Domestic Happiness

Lost Time

In 1998, the King of Bhutan declared that the country's goal was to attain the highest possible level of gross national happiness. But in 1999, he committed a fatal mistake: he lifted the ban on owning a television set. Rupert Murdoch quickly supplied forty-six channels via his satellite network Star TV. And so the inhabitants of the kingdom could see the usual lot of sex, violence, advertising and serials that the inhabitants of the rich countries were also watching. The result was not long in coming: divorces, criminality and drug use immediately shot up.[1]

Bhutan, a small country nestled between India and China, experienced in a short space of time a transition that had lasted several decades in the rich countries. In France and the United States, television was almost non-existent in the 1950s. Today there are at least two TV sets per household. Americans spend on average almost five hours a day in front of their TVs. Europeans spend an hour less. For Robert Putnam, the renowned sociologist at Harvard University, television is the principal cause of the decline of the

American civil spirit. Being stuck too long in front of the set leads to neglecting friends, family, clubs and associations – all that he calls 'social capital'.[2]

Television offers immediate gratification to the viewer, to the detriment of pastimes that require learning, like playing a musical instrument. But it is a pleasure that is soon regretted. All the studies show that screen entertainment is one of the most frustrating leisure pastimes for the viewers themselves. The correlation between the number of hours spent watching TV and any measure of satisfaction is negative: 'Like other compulsive or addictive behaviours, television seems to be a surprisingly unsatisfying experience', writes Putnam. According to the available studies, despite the time devoted to it, television satisfaction is far behind other leisure pursuits. Americans rank it after ironing clothes! Economists have identified this problem as that of 'time inconsistency of preferences': humans are given to activities that they later regret having practised![3] The person I am today is not what I would like to be tomorrow. For example, I would like to stop drinking, but I cannot manage to do it. I would like to read the book rather than watch the TV series, but I cannot manage that, either. To speak the language of psychoanalysts, humans are torn between the 'id' that seeks immediate gratification, and the 'superego' that pushes for deferred satisfactions that lift us above ourselves. Psychologists have even identified two regions of the brain: the limbic system for immediate satisfaction, and the lateral prefrontal cortex (the calculating part of the brain) for deferred satisfactions.[4] Two distinct parts of our being are competing for our attention.

But television does more than supply immediate gratifications: it transforms our gaze upon the world and into ourselves. TV characters are beautiful and rich. After a suicide on television, it has been demonstrated that the real suicide rate also increases. When a group of women are shown top models, their morale significantly drops! The impact of feminine standards as fixed by fashion magazines has been studied in France by Fabrice Etilé, who shows that it causes persistent misery. Claudia Senik speaks of 'hopeless comparisons' of one's own life to that of figures who cannot be imitated (stars and celebrities) – but sometimes also to those close to us who have succeeded better than we have.[5]

Television and advertising play on an essential aspect of human nature: the pathological need to compare oneself with others. A person can genuinely cry at the misfortune of someone else, and yet simultaneously be envious of the person who succeeds better than he does. In a laboratory experiment where people are asked about their preferences, the students at an American university respond that they would prefer to earn $50,000 when their fellow students earn $25,000, rather than earn $100,000 when the others earn $200,000. The results of this experiment are observed in real life. Happiness depends on comparisons that each person establishes with a reference group, whether friends or colleagues. In American families, an astonishing observation has been made: a wife will have a greater probability of working if her sister's husband earns more than her own husband. In effect, she must compensate for the lack of earning power she feels vis-à-vis her own sister.

But fortunately human rivalry does not extend across all dimensions. It disappears in leisure, for example. The same American college students were asked to choose between two options: (1) you have two weeks vacation and your colleagues only one, or (2) you have four weeks vacation and the others eight; they all chose the second option, that of spending four weeks on holiday. No mimetic behaviour is being observed here. Rivalry bears only on visible traits of social success. The silent happiness of others – here about free time – does not sharpen competitiveness.

The economist Bruno Frey has proposed a very useful classification to understand the mechanisms at work when people compare themselves to others. He suggests distinguishing between 'extrinsic goods' and 'intrinsic goods'.[6] The former relate to status and wealth: these are the external signs of social success, the social heritage that is accumulated over the course of time that marks everybody's place in society. *Intrinsic* goods are linked to the affection of others (relatedness), to love, to the feeling of having a purpose in life. These are experiences 'in flux', which change with passing time. *Extrinsic* goods sharpen social rivalry, while intrinsic goods augment wellbeing, but silently.

Unless you are a saint or a socialite (Schopenhauer said: without being either 'Stoic or Machiavellian'), both kinds of goods are certainly necessary in order to be happy. But the problem is that it is hard to understand one's own emotions, and we systematically underestimate the benefits of intrinsic goods. Many people dream of a mansion and therefore choose to move out of the city centre to find a better ratio between quality and price in real estate. But they forget the psychological cost of commuting and often end up (without wanting to admit it) regretting their choice.

Why is it so hard to understand what is good for you? Daniel Kahneman, a psychologist by training who got the Nobel Prize in economics, has taken up this question. He shows that we tend to retain only two moments: the most intense and the last. Of vacations, I remember the farewells when going home and the most exciting day. Everything else vanishes in the halo of life that is past. This 'peak/end' model makes us forget intermediary moments.[7] Doing so, projecting into the future, people tend also to ignore experienced duration. They project themselves into 'peak' experiences to the detriment of others in the 'strong flow'. Memory has a hard time retaining the silent emotions of ordinary days. Marcel Proust's genius in his novel *In Search of Lost Time* is to show the struggle in oneself to get beyond the ordinary propensity to retain only the outstanding moments. 'Lost time' has the double sense of past time that you think you have forgotten, and the time you think you lost in doing futile things that are nevertheless essential.

Divorcing and Ageing

Another fundamental trait of human nature is its incredible capacity for adaptation. Polar bears and brown bears form two distinct species. Humans, by contrast, undertook long migrations both north and south; they did not mutate, but instead adapted. Inuits and Pygmies belong to the same human species, they can mate and have children. In the realm of human psychology, research has long noted this essential trait of adapting to life's events, whether happy or tragic.[8] Whatever the ordeal a person may experience, the indicators of satisfaction quickly return to their initial levels.

A person seems to get used to everything, which is both reassuring and depressing. Thus across time and space, the percentages of happy and unhappy people are remarkably stable.[9] This stability obviously owes a lot to humans' formidable capacity of adaptation and imitation. Any wealth or any progress is relative, and quickly dissolves in a comparison with others. When millionaires are asked about the size of the fortune necessary to make them feel 'truly at ease', they all respond in the same way, whatever the level of income they have already attained: they need double what they already possess! The heart of the problem is that people do not anticipate their own capacity to adapt. They think that they might be happy if they were given (a little) more and then they would be satisfied, but they are not. The rise in income *to come* always makes one dream, although once it is achieved, this rise is never sufficient. For people compare their *future* income to their *current* aspirations, without taking into account the ineluctable evolution of the aspirations. This is the principal key to the vain quest for happiness.[10] For Kant, 'happiness is not an ideal of reason, but of the imagination'.[11]

Given the average stability of levels of happiness, though, there exist certain essential parameters that affect it systematically. The relation between happiness and age is the most surprising. It resembles a U-curve: the young and the seniors are (much) happier than adults of intermediate ages. From 25 to 50 years of age, happiness constantly shrinks, before rising back up. One finds at age 70 the happiness of a young person of 30. At 80, one has rediscovered (on average) the joy of being 18! How can we make sense of this astonishing graph? Perhaps economists are not best placed to answer this question, but the distinction proposed by Bruno Frey helps us grasp what is in play. Old age liberates us from a huge weight, that of accumulating useless goods, and allows us to give their place back to intrinsic goods.

Rabelais puts in the mouth of one of his characters this question: 'What shall be the end of so many trials and tribulations?' The answer given is: 'That when we return we shall sit down, rest, and be merry.'[12] Old age opens us to the pleasure of simple 'duration', of passing time that is intrinsically valuable. Milan Kundera in *Testaments Betrayed* (1993) marvels at the 'crepuscular' late work of Beethoven. In the evening of his life, the master composed sonatas that broke the traditional codes of composition. According to Kundera, this is the work of a genius liberated from the weight of having to be one, of having to please.

Two other factors are predominant in all ages and on all continents. Whatever the situations of interviewees, divorce and the loss of a job reduce happiness by considerable proportions. These are the moments that send individuals back to solitude and to doubts about their own identity, which may make them despair. François de Singly has well described the shock represented by divorce for the person who is abandoned. The 'ego', supposed sovereign master of individual decisions, no longer amount to anything when the partner has gone.

One is tempted to say that it is not necessary to go much further to understand the modern world: divorce *and* job loss are its two most striking traits. Is the concomitant rise of these two miseries, in two such different registers, a coincidence? It is difficult to believe so. But what would be the logical connection? How can we have concocted a society that multiplies those events that so increase widespread malaise?

Alain Ehrenberg supplies a useful key to interpretation (although generally speaking he contrasts France and the United States, the answers in this domain are perfectly concordant). A modern individual aspires to autonomy, to the freedom of realizing a destiny worthy of his or her expectations. But along the way he or she discovers an unforeseen obstacle: competition with others. Tocqueville made the same observation about American society in a strong chapter explicitly titled 'Why Americans are so restless in the midst of their prosperity':

> When all the prerogatives of birth and fortune are destroyed and all the professions are open to everyone and a person can reach the top of any of them on his own, ambitious men may readily conclude that the road to success is wide and smooth and easily imagine illustrious futures for themselves. [. . . However] not only are they powerless by themselves, but at every step they encounter huge obstacles that they failed at first to notice. Having destroyed the obstructing privileges enjoyed by some of their fellow men, they run up against universal competition.(trans. Arthur Goldhammer)

For an economist, competition is *a priori* a good thing. It is customary since Adam Smith to explain that it makes the price of merchandise drop and increases the purchasing power of consumers. On the employment market, competition is supposed to enable a better matching of employees to their employers. But does this line of reasoning hold good for private life? Should we believe that couples divorce because 'matrimonial competition' increases the possibility of their finding a better partner? Gary Becker, Nobel Laureate in economics, thinks so.[13] In *A Treatise on the Family*, one of the most important of postwar writings, he analyses marriage as the search for a partner in an 'imperfect market' that is subject to the costs of learning and rupture, and aims at the efficacy of the encounter, i.e. mating. The result (marriage) remains in suspension, however, due to the discovery of 'better' opportunities that would improve the efficacy of the matching. Studies of happiness show that divorce resembles more a zero-sum game: the one who is abandoned loses the happiness battle. The virtues of a competitive world are no longer valid when one is the losing party.

Make Your Own Unhappiness

Aspirants to happiness often believe they are disciples of Epicurus, who agreed with the modern idea (notably propounded by Jeremy Bentham in the eighteenth century) that one should seek pleasure and avoid pain.[14] But Epicurus takes great care to distinguish pleasures 'in movement', which are linked to the satisfaction of a need and hence mixed with pain, and pleasures 'in repose', which are static, pure, and presuppose that desires have been satisfied.[15] Plato in *The Gorgias* is more radical. The search for happiness suffers from a fundamental contradiction: happiness requires desire, yet desire excludes happiness. For Plato, happiness (if it can be called that) is the recompense for a 'good life', not its goal. A good life (*eudaimonia*) means finding one's place in the human world, like a star that turns in harmony around another. Aristotle prudently concludes that since the specificities of what is human are reason and virtue, 'hence [a person's] life does not need pleasure to be added [to virtuous activity] as some sort of extra decoration; rather, it has its pleasure within itself'.[16]

Economists have long objected to the distinction between vulgar pleasures and those that uplift the soul. People who understand the beauty of a work of art are certainly happier than others. The effort that has to be devoted to understand the artistic force of an opera is repaid by a greater happiness in experiencing it, like an investment. But this does not create a qualitative difference between opera and television, only a difference in degree. Richard Layard, a disciple of Bentham, willingly admitted that variables such as purpose in life and positive relations with others and with oneself count for a lot in an individual's happiness. But why should they be opposed to the search for other, more trivial satisfactions, like having a nice car or a nice apartment? The happiness of going to a brothel might be compared with that of going to church, given that the same person can do both and calibrate the time spent in each. Everything is a question of doses.

Like a sovereign who possesses all the power levers, Homo Economicus is supposed to choose freely, according to this model, between good and evil, between time spent working and time spent lazing around. But who believes that? Far from keeping accounts of his affects, any person is a composite of diverse personalities that cohabit more or less harmoniously. You can be going to a meeting that is essential for your career and yet you jump into the water to save someone who is drowning. No calculation is at work. Due to the force of emotion, you jump from one state to another. In his book *Is Capitalism Moral?* Andre Comte-Sponville[17] has proposed a useful typology that is inspired by Blaise Pascal's theory of three powers, which distinguished between the body, reason and the heart ('that has its reasons that Reason does not know'). Comte-Sponville proposes four categories: economics, politics, morality and love. Each has its own rationale. A mother who takes care of her children *only* out of duty would be a bad mother. A politician who depended on morality to guide his or her actions would make a poor leader. Similarly, economics has its rules, those of calculation and profit-seeking, which are distinct from those of morality or politics.

Even within the choices that are supposed to be economic and rational there persist aspects of ourselves in conflict. I might want to save money in order to prepare for my retirement or the future of my children, and yet I cannot manage to do so, spending 'in spite of myself' the household savings. Inside us live beings that confront each other, veritable Dr Jekylls and Mr Hydes, inseparable twins who hate each other. The concern to live according to an ideal does battle against the desire for immediate gratifications that depart from that ideal. How can we teach them to coexist? The famous example of Ulysses and the Sirens gives an illustration of the possible methods. For Jon Elster, who famously commented on this passage of the *Odyssey*,[18] what Ulysses had to do was 'rationally manage his irrationality'. I know my temptations (yielding to the Siren songs) and so I manage by anticipating them and tying to the mast the person I do not want to become. If I am on a diet to lose weight, I will avoid passing in front of a pastry shop. I should save to prepare for my old age, I will put my money in a savings account I cannot touch, and thus avoid spending it. I struggle against the human being I might become if I yielded. The Homo Economicus who lives inside me is hard-working. He maximizes utility – but does not know whose.

An Anthropological Monster

Who is Homo Economicus? Originally he was a fiction invented by economists. Their model was a character from the novel *Robinson Crusoe* by Daniel Defoe, imagined as a metaphor for an Englishman discovering a virgin land (in all senses of the term – with no inhabitants, no past, on the American model) and leading a 'rational' life. The British economist Lionel Robbins presented Homo Economicus' mission in the 1930s: to allocate in an efficient way the scarce resources he possesses. Defined in these terms, economic analysis includes all possible kinds of arbitration: time spent sleeping and being awake, the duration of work and of leisure; the production of consumer goods (in Crusoe's case, fish) versus investment goods (making fishing rods). In all circumstances, Robinson Crusoe tried to maximize his wellbeing, like a firm that maximizes its profits. This ceaseless rationality led the sociologist Pierre Bourdieu to say that, as so described, Homo Economicus is 'an anthropological monster'.

Of course economists are not the dupes of the narrative weaknesses of their hero, any more than are philosophers when they expound the ideas of Descartes on the *cogito* or those of Hegel on the *spirit*. Their foremost ambition is to understand the logic of economic calculation, to find out where and when it should be applied, using the reasoning 'all other things being equal' (their favourite expression). The results of experimental psychology are in this respect rather reassuring. It seems that there exist many distinct spheres of human activity that would merit separate examination, each having its own logic.

The reign of Homo Economicus in his kingdom is quite delicate, however. The principal characteristic ascribed to him is to be rational. What does that mean? In a word: that he prefers more to less, an approximation that does not appear unreasonable, but which poses formidable problems. One might certainly accept that I prefer 1,000 euros to 100, and 100 euros to 10, and hence *a fortiori* that I also prefer 1,000 euros to 10. This 'transitivity' of human choices is the foundation of rationality as defined by economists. But does it apply to other choices than a quantum of money? I might prefer Anne to Catherine and Catherine to Martine, but does that imply necessarily that I prefer Anne to Martine? That is the question; the 'rational' answer according to economists is necessarily 'yes'. But everybody knows that this is not necessarily the case, which 'proves' that love is not rational. In another domain, where emotions play a lesser role: tennis player A might beat player B and player B beat C, without it following that A necessarily beats C. Nadal beats Federer who beats Djokovic. But Djokovic beats Nadal. All tennis fans know why: Federer is the best except against left-handers. Djokovic does not have this problem and plays as well against a left-hander (Nadal) as against a right-hander.

Another example of this absence of 'transitivity' is given by what is called the paradox of Condorcet. The political theorist showed that the rationality of each individual cannot be conjugated into the rationality of the ensemble. I may be rational, like my neighbours to the right and left. But the three of us form an inconsequential ensemble. For example, if voting on a colour, we might prefer blue to white, white to red, and yet also prefer red to blue, at two against three each time. No doubt the risk of collective inconsistency explains why the model of representative democracy has prevailed in practice. It allows people to delegate to a 'rational' executive the responsibility for exercising power.

But the Condorcet Paradox also illuminates the irrationality of individuals themselves. If there are several beings inside us who compete for our attention, it will be difficult to get them to agree. Each part of our being might have an internal coherence: the alcoholic will prefer more wine than less, while the sober self prefers the opposite. The being that we want to be has to reconcile them. It will want sometimes to limit its choices and to set aside 'dangerous' alternatives. Thus the conflict between the search for immediate gratification and the concern for the long term testifies to the difficulty of being 'reasonable'. Economists have long thought that the problem was simply to arbitrate between one reward today and another one tomorrow. If you ask me: 'Do you want 100 euros tomorrow or else 200 in a year and a day?', I will answer '200 euros in a year and a day'. The return is advantageous, and so I willingly delay the reward until later. But if one proposes '100 euros immediately or 200 euros in a year', then I am going to answer: 100 euros now, even if the distance in time has not changed between the two options (one year in both cases). For the present moment addresses an individual other than the one I wanted to be yesterday, someone who wants everything 'right away'.[19] If I understand my own temptations, I will arrange 'in advance' not to be offered the choice to oblige myself to take the 200 euros in a year while foregoing the 100 euros now. Like Ulysses, I would seek to tie myself to a mast to lift myself above my condition – as an alcoholic, a deviant, a voracious person.

Fortunately, I am not alone. Society helps me to manage the hardest decisions. Old age and sickness insurance are obligatory, just like educating children. The United States, which leaves a greater individual choice than do European societies in this domain, is also the country where the greatest poverty is observed, for this very reason. And the resounding American economic failure in the year 2008 related in large part to the absurd way in which the most precarious people were pushed into indebtedness. Financial deregulation did everything possible to incite American households to use credit cards or else contract mortgages beyond their means. In effect, the country released Ulysses from the mast, and so America drowned.

Ten Pieces of Advice

Beyond the institutions that support the social existence of us all, we must also reflect on the best way we may individually live the social game, especially in periods of crisis like the one we are currently experiencing. Bruno Frey has taken up the challenge (with bravura) of giving lessons for living, which may be understood as lessons in caution.[20] There is some irony in advising others how to act in this most individual realm, but the tips merit being quoted, if only to illuminate the efforts that have to be made to resist the persistent counter-currents exerted by social experience. Here are his ten pieces of advice (they are not commandments but the best way for individuals to play the social game):

1. Do not worry about not being a genius, since geniuses are not happier than other people. One of the secrets of happiness can be simply summarized: compare yourself to those who have *less* (of whatever) than you. On average, those with bronze medals are happier than silver medallists (which has been statistically verified). Silver medallists compare themselves to gold medallists. Bronze medallists compare themselves to those who have none.

2. Earn money – but without making this a disease. Any increase in salary makes people happy – but only for a few months. In less than a year, 40 per cent of the pleasure has already evaporated, and you have to earn even more to find satisfaction in money.

3. Age with grace. Provided that your health is up to it, growing old does not damage happiness. On the contrary, like Beethoven you may find pleasure as a senior with new creativity, freed from the constraint of seeking recognition.

4. Do not compare yourself with others in matters of beauty. Norms are unrealistic. The pressures that top models exert on your psyche create useless frustration.
5. 'Believe' in something: whether God, social justice, or the beauty of nature. Life needs a meaning for you to be happy and escape from yourself.
6. Help others: altruism turns you away from yourself, and this does you good (for the same reasons).
7. Control your desires. New 'aspirations' always exceed 'realizations', as elevated as the latter may be.
8. Keep your friends: they are the beings dearest to you, even if they are the least visible.
9. Live as a couple, for solitude is not good.
10. Accept what you are; rationally control your weaknesses. If you procrastinate, understand it and fix yourself some rules. But inversely, if you are psycho-rigid, then force yourself to do forbidden things.

These pieces of advice may seem charmingly naive. They also annoy psychoanalysts, who see the problem as a psychic conflict that no peaceful resolution will ever solve. But Frey's list has the great merit of showing how society pushes each of us to follow almost the inverse of these precepts: by comparing yourself to Steve Jobs, to athletes, to top models – in short, everything pushes us to make our own unhappiness.

However, beyond individual choices, it is the organization of society that is today being questioned, starting with the most important factor: the organization of work.

2

Work: A Diminishing Value

Management by Stress

After divorce, the loss of a job is the other great factor in the ever-creeping suffering in the modern world. In studies in the USA, workers who are 'absolutely certain' they will keep their job are significantly happier than others. Everything points to the evolution of the working world as aiming to reduce the happiness found there. Since the financial revolution of the 1980s, a decisive break has occurred, creating a new kind of misery inside the world of the workplace. 'Industrial' capitalism funded on implicit cooperation between labour and capital has been replaced by a 'financial' capitalism that is freed from the rules of the 'social economy of the market' prevailing after the Second World War.

Yesterday, work was an integrating factor. The large industrial corporations offered the promise of promotion at all levels of the hierarchy. Shop-floor workers could hope to become foremen, and foremen to become administrators . . . Today, firms try to be lean – constantly thinner – like fashion models. They outsource jobs to their subcontractors, emptying employees' jobs and services of the implicit protections that firms previously gave to their workers. Yesterday, management schools taught future business leaders the ways to diversify their industrial activities. The idea was to protect the firm from the shocks of any conjuncture by having several realms of activity. Today, the same schools teach the art of specializing in niche sectors and outsourcing all other jobs to near or distant subcontractors.

One might believe that these strategies aim to make firms more efficient. But that is not necessarily the case, at least if we understand 'efficient' in the ordinary sense of performing better, because by externalizing tasks, one also reduces synergies. A study of airline companies in the United States showed that those that possessed their own terminal were better equipped than the others, as well as less likely to have flight delays and cancellations. However, those that subcontracted the management of their terminals were in fact more *profitable*, even if they weren't more efficient, for they could push down the costs. By externalizing tasks, the purchaser who places the order can blackmail the subcontractors and put on pressure to keep rates down. These results have been confirmed by other studies in other sectors.[1]

For the same reasons, conglomerates (groups that operate in several sectors of activity) are often attacked on the stock exchange. They are reputed to be less profitable than specialized firms. But the method of calculation plays a crucial role in these evaluations. A conglomerate tends to save the subsidiaries of its own group that are in difficulty, which otherwise would go bankrupt and disappear from the accounting figures. The conglomerate is no less 'efficient' in the productivity sense of the term; it is even generally more so, but it is less profitable (like the airline companies that manage their own terminals).

Nowadays, management methods that encourage firms to specialize, to resort to subcontracting or to delocalization, are not seeking technical efficiency but profit. It is in the name of the same logic that relations in the workplace have been transformed over the last thirty years. In the lean world of modern firms, cooperation and reciprocity have become rarer. Rivalry among staff within the same company is encouraged. The famous boss of General Electric, Jack Welch, did not hesitate to set the tone: each year, he fired 10 per cent of his employees to keep up the 'hunger' of the remaining staff. This is called 'management by stress'.

Thus a new kind of moral suffering afflicts the business world. How can we interpret it? Companies have always been governed by a single principle: efficiency. They do not have 'moral' concerns. The famous Chicago economist Milton Friedman summarized this process in the celebrated phrase 'The social responsibility of the enterprise is to make a profit.' There is no moral concern present in that.[2]

Andre Comte-Sponville also poses the question of morality in his book on capitalism. His answer is that capitalism is neither moral nor immoral. It obeys another logic: it is *amoral*. 'The business of business is business', to paraphrase Milton Friedman again. Just like a mother who takes care of her child *only* 'out of duty' would be a bad mother, a company that arranged its business affairs in the name of morality would be a bad company. One should act out of self-interest, out of duty, or else out of love, according to the case, but nothing is more deplorable than to want to mingle the kinds of motivations. When a company claims to be behaving morally, it really always does so for commercial reasons – or out of a desire for efficiency.

Nevertheless, it is in moral terms that employees call attention to their suffering in the workplace. Companies are not like a supermarket where one tries to find the best relation between quality and price. They are the link to interpersonal relations that obey their own laws. In a supermarket, the consumer is faced with objects whose specific function, said Marx in his theory of 'commodity fetishism', is to mask the social and human conditions that have enabled them to be produced. There the consumer incarnates the Homo Economicus, a cold and rational animal that thinks of nothing but his self-interest. But a company whose organization was founded on the single idea that its employees would live in some egotistic bubble would lose the benefits of the cooperation and reciprocity of which the employees are capable towards each other.[3]

A laboratory experiment illustrates what is in play. In the 'Trust Game' two people who cannot see each other and do not know each other (each hidden behind a computer screen) are confronted with the following situation. The first day, the sender (S) finds himself offered the sum of $50 at the start of the experiment. He can leave immediately with it, in which case the experiment is terminated. Or he can send all (or part) of that sum to the other player, the receiver (R). In this case, the experimenter multiplies by three the sum sent. (R) can leave with this, and the game is suspended. But he too may send all or part of his gain back to (S), and the game is then actually terminated.[4]

A rational economic agent who is faced with this game ought to reason as follows: If I send 'my' dollars to the other agent, he will receive triple the sum, but what interest would he have in sending any money back to me? None, since he doesn't know me and will never meet me. If he, too, is rational, he has no interest in being kind to me. Knowing that, I send nothing. But what is the actual result of the experiment? Obviously, the opposite. A large majority of participants send part of the money that is given to them, and in two-thirds of all cases are recompensed for it. Why send money when this is useless? Traditional economic reasoning has no answer. Running counter to economic calculation, the game shows that most often humans do indeed respond to the confidence that has been placed in them.[5]

Psychologists speak of reciprocity, a concept halfway between altruism and individualism, to refer to the desire to enter into contact (if only in thought) with others.[6] For their part, anthropologists since Marcel Mauss have identified the logic of gift and counter-gift. If I give someone a present, I oblige them, in the noble sense of the term, to make me a counter-gift. But this is not an exchange, since another dimension is solicited, a 'logic of honour' that is never interrupted. The person who first offered a gift receives the counter-gift, and is in turn obliged by the latter. Contrary to the exchange that concludes with the transaction itself, the gift/counter-gift sequence opens a chain of reciprocity that is never broken.[7]

A company that ignored this spontaneous tendency among its employees to reciprocity and cooperation would fail in its moral obligation, in Friedman's sense. It is in its interest to take into account the moral behaviour of its employees. At this point in the reasoning, we find again the argument offered by Andre Comte-Sponville: while the company does not itself have moral behaviour, it may sometimes exploit for its own ends the moral behaviours of its employees, whose rationale is quite other. In that case, employees are allowed to work in harmony with their moral sentiments, while in a company that ignores them, they are being paid (or threatened) to ignore these sentiments.

The New Spirit of Capitalism

In this way, a 'new spirit of capitalism' is born, one that creates a kind of cognitive break within the business world. What 'human' relationship is it possible to have when each colleague is a rival for power, when how you perform tasks is constantly assessed, which installs mistrust between employees and their superiors in the hierarchy? The example of blood donors mentioned in the Introduction illustrates the difficulty of making the moral and the market values of work cohabit. Another example cited by Maya Beauvallet[8] also illustrates these difficulties. In an Israeli day-care centre, the director wanted to combat the constant delays of parents in picking up their children at the end of the day. To remedy the situation, he decided to institute a tax: from now on, parents would pay ten dollars each hour they were late. The result was not long in coming. To the stupefaction of the director, starting the next day, the number of tardy parents tripled! The explanation was simple (and the same as for blood donors): before the tax, parents tried to be on time in the name of an imperative that could be called 'moral' – so as not to shame their children and/or not to inconvenience the teachers. As soon as they were given a penalty, they immediately changed the scale of values to which they related their actions. They now calculated that ten dollars an hour was the cost of a baby-sitter.[9]

The director who levied ten dollars an hour for lateness and the director of the blood donation centre who wanted to increase the number of donors by offering them a prize were both committing the same mistake in reasoning. They both thought that an economic incentive might be added to a moral incentive. What they discovered was something altogether different: financial reward does not *add* its effects to moral reward, but eliminates the latter. The same person might have moral behaviour or interested calculations according to circumstances, but cannot have both at the same time. A friend walks you home to avoid your having to take a taxi, but if you thank him by giving him the cost of the taxi fare that he allowed you to save, then you will lose him as a friend.

Jean Tirole and Roland Benabou have analysed a related question:[10] Should parents encourage their children to work hard at school by promising them a reward if they get good grades? Tirole and Benabou offer a 'rational' response. A child to whom his parents promise a reward will necessarily ask himself 'Why are they doing that?' And the 'rational' child, according to these two economists, will conclude 'Because I am not up to it . . . If my own parents offer me a reward to incite me to get good marks, it is because they know that I do not have the necessary abilities.' And the 'rational' child will lose courage. He will think, 'I lack the drive.' So sometimes it is better to abstain from offering monetary rewards, since they might demoralize the recipient.

This type of reasoning (which is itself a model of intelligence) transforms a question of affect into one of interested calculation. Another and simpler response is possible. 'If my parents offer me a reward, it is because they do not love me. They treat me like an employee for their own desires, and perhaps they would even be capable of withdrawing their affection from me if I do not succeed.' Monetary incentives become counter-productive when they overthrow the register of affects. Fortunately, not all parents fall into this trap. Often a reward – a gift to celebrate a good score – comes without being announced in advance, and is given after the fact and for the pleasure of it. But for an economist, a reward is only useful if it is anticipated. In the inverse case, a child will spontaneously understand that her parents simply want to share her joy, and everything goes back to normal: it comes from love, not economic calculation.

All human societies rest on some institutions that encourage cooperation and on others that sharpen competition. They differ in the articulation of these two registers, but all societies resort to them. The livelier the intensity of competition, then the more institutions charged with facing it tend to promote solidarity. Claude Levi-Strauss, noting the quasi-universality of the ban on incest, explained that the exchange of women is constitutive of social relations because it also obliges families to be open to others, and in this way pacifies their inter-relations ('marry or kill'). But the sociologist Max Weber had another view. In his eyes, the ban on incest aimed at pacifying families within themselves because it omits sisters from the rivalry between sons and fathers. Families want to reduce their internal rivalries (and Freud would add that this is no doubt the cause of other pathologies) in order better to tackle those rivalries they must confront outside.

Coming back to economic matters, the work of Oliver Williamson (the Nobel Prize-Winner in Economics in 2009), starting with his first book *Markets and Hierarchies* (1975), has clearly shown that capitalism is the articulation of two types of institutions whose logics are very different. We have to distinguish between anonymous markets that induce competitive behaviour aiming to supply the best ratio between quality and price, and businesses that obey another logic altogether. Within a company, the employees are habitually in solidarity with each other in the face of competitors and of clients – in short, in the face of the market environment. When this protection is lost, the workers live under a new and constant competitive pressure, which may entail among the most vulnerable of them often insurmountable woes.

Maya Beauvallet has detected a surprising number of cases in which the search for increased efficiency through bonuses has backfired against the instigators.[11] Imagine that a target goal is given to teachers and that they receive a bonus pegged to the success of their students in high-school examinations. What are they going to do? Two 'rational' things: (1) ignore the best pupils, who are sure of succeeding, or (2) ignore the worst students, who have no chance of passing anyway! Thus the teachers will target their efforts on those who are just 'below the bar'. This is not a very interesting strategy for society as a whole, since the school would not take an interest in the majority of its students.

Another example illustrates the same problem: the attempt to privatize prisons. In the United States, private prisons sign a contract with a state and keep the profits of their corresponding management of prison facilities. The result is that they are more profitable – which is not surprising – but why? Because they employ guards who are less qualified, less well paid. The use of force is five times more frequent: almost ten times more injuries are suffered in private than in state prisons. Despite the 463 indicators specified in the contract, the 'quality' of the prisoners' rights remains vague.

In making 'the concern to do well' disappear as a spring of human actions, companies are led to increasingly implement bonuses and penalties. In the case of the day-care director, he would have had to put a much higher tariff on lateness (say 50 euros an hour) for his method to work. When the business world breaks 'work value', it must organize a more unequal world to function effectively. It must increase the rewards and harden the penalties.

The New Age of Inequalities

The golden age of business conceived as a large family occurred in the postwar era, with the spread of what is called Fordism. The 'Detroit Treaty' – the name given by *Fortune* magazine to the salary compromise signed between the United Auto Workers (UAW) and General Motors – which had guaranteed workers' salary increases at the pace of productivity gains, quickly spread to other companies. Non-unionized workers profited from it, too, since company directors wanted to prevent unionization where it had not already occurred. Thus, in the 1950s, workers caught up a good share of their salary lag compared to office workers. This was the golden age of managerial capitalism, which was incarnated in France in the 'Thirty Glorious Years', the period of prosperity after the end of the Second World War.

In 1981 the election of Ronald Reagan opened a new chapter in the history of capitalism. Upon his arrival in the White House, he broke a strike by air traffic controllers and launched a formidable challenge to the power of labour unions. It was the start of a 're-engineering' of companies that broke the postwar social compromise. Union power crumbled. Workers were forced out of their bastions. Walmart, the big box chain, replaced General Motors as the largest American employer. Walmart employees earned $20,000 a year, half as much (after correcting for inflation) as GM workers were earning a year earlier.[12]

In his book *The Conscience of a Liberal* (2007), Paul Krugman accurately described the rupture that was produced in the United States in the 1980s: 'Postwar America was, above all, a middle-class society [. . . a] relatively equal society with a strong middle class and an equable political scene'. From the standpoint of the 1950s and 1960s, America, like Europe at the same time, could believe it had achieved a golden age, when prosperity was shared equitably in a country cemented by a middle class that was strong both economically and morally.

Yet the idea so firmly anchored in the American imaginary, that (as Cullen Murphy puts it) 'for America, the middle class is the core social fact – our gyroscope, our ballast, our compass',[13] did in fact not take place until much later. Following the rise in power of American capitalism from 1870 to 1929, there was no spontaneous tendency towards the emergence of a 'middle class' (in the sense this would assume in the 1950s) to be actually discerned during this period. The phenomenon that economists would call the 'Great Compression', which suddenly reduced inequalities, occurred after the Second World War. This is when 'mentalities' appear to have suddenly changed, fostering a society with more solidarity. The Cold War paradoxically maintained this spirit because the anti-Communist phobia of the

McCarthy period ironically reinforced the 'Communist' traits of American society: egalitarianism and promotion of the working class.

But with the 1980s, a new rupture took place. The income of the poorest 10 per cent eroded by almost 60 per cent compared to the levels reached in the 1960s, while the income of the richest 10 per cent increased by 80 per cent, and those in the top percentile quintupled their income! Starting in the middle of the 1980s, the process that accelerated inequalities has widened to the whole society.[14] It is no longer the reflection of working-class impoverishment, but touches all social layers. For example, individuals who are *a priori* close in their years of education or professional experience sometimes see their fates diverge in totally unpredictable ways. According to the sector of activity or the firm where they started work, the salary gaps might become considerable, even for two graduates of the same school and of the same age. This factor is called 'residual inequalities', which seems to relate to life chance more than to achievements. In the course of the 1990s, this process explained two-thirds of the rise in salary gaps.

The shockwave of inequalities is amplified within families. The American ideal of a woman in the home whose 'husband brings home the bacon' by working from nine to five has been abandoned. Now both husbands and wives work more frequently, which is not a problem in itself. What becomes problematic is that social endogamy (marrying within one's social stratum) was also reinforced during this period. Now the two spouses tend to be much closer socially than they were previously. The labour market and the matrimonial market pull in the same direction, that of a growing stratification of society. At the bottom of the new poverty, single-parent families incarnate the problem of abandonment. They suffer twice over. They count on a single revenue instead of two, and they do not have social insurance when facing unemployment, which is implicitly derived from the spouse's salary. Their income is low and their risk is high. The single-parent family in the working-class milieu has become the symbol of modern pauperization.[15]

The Hyper-Class

Starting in the 1990s, inequalities broke through another threshold. The data gathered by Thomas Piketty and Emmanuel Saez offer a striking portrait of the role taken by what they call the 'working rich' – in contrast to the 'working poor' – a category that appeared in the 1980s.[16] While the richest one-hundredth of Americans earned seven per cent of the total income at the start of the 1970s, they now earned almost a quarter of the total income in the USA. At the start of the twenty-first century, they outstripped the share that had been theirs a century earlier, in the Gilded Age.[17] A sort of salary putsch occurred in a silent way.

The work of Thomas Philippon in the USA and Olivier Godechot in France shows that the rise of inequalities is intimately tied to the role played by finance in the national economy. In ten years, financiers have seen their remuneration multiply nine-fold! Between 1996 and 2006, the rise in the pay of the top group, the one earning more than a million euros a year, is more of the wealthy than half accounted for by the remunerations offered in the world of finance. In the United Kingdom, the corresponding figure is 70 per cent.[18]

Directors of the major corporations have also benefited from this inflation of the payscale. In ten years, from 1996 to 2006, company directors, apart from finance, registered a tripling of their income (less of course than financiers, but six times more than film actors, for example). Previously, directors' pay was indexed to that of their employees. In a famous maxim, the banker John Pierpont Morgan explained at the start of the previous century that he would not trust a company whose boss earned twenty times more than his employees. This indexing would long be the case in both France and the USA.

The years from 1980 to 2010 broke this unwritten rule. Over the whole period, the salary of directors multiplied by ten! Seeking sometimes to justify the abrupt soaring of their remuneration, they claimed that this hike was merited by their increased effectiveness. The very notion of the 'working rich' is ambiguous, and some might see it as a sort of apologetics.[19] The book *Pay without Performance*, though, shows that the real break relates more to *how* they are paid than to managerial results.[20] Company directors set their own salaries, directly or indirectly, through the auditing committees they themselves choose. The tie with performance is stretched, even when it is not simply inverted.

According to Krugman's formula, 'The question of how much to pay a top executive has a strong element of subjectivity, even fashion, to it.' The only constraint is of a moral order: not to arouse indignation among employees, in the media, or with regulatory authorities. This constraint disappeared in the 1980s. 'Since the 1970s, norms and institutions in the United States have changed in a direction that either encouraged or permitted sharply higher inequality.' Each person compares him or herself to colleagues, neighbours, friends. For example, French company directors compare themselves to those in other countries – Germany, Britain or America. Yet real mobility is rather weak. One finds few French bosses directing foreign companies, or foreign bosses working in France. The subjective force of these comparisons, however, seems to suffice to overturn payscales. CEOs approach and outstrip the salary scales of entertainment stars. As Piketty and Saez summarize it: 'The hike in income of directors is a social fact before it is an economic fact.'[21]

A hyper-class has been born that has tended gradually to free itself from common judgement. Robert Frank, a reporter with the *Wall Street Journal*, writes in *Richistan*: 'The rich weren't just getting richer; they were becoming financial foreigners, creating their own country within a country, their own society within a society, their economy within an economy.'[22] F. Scott Fitzgerald made the same observation in the 1920s: 'The rich are different from you and me.' Thierry Pech humorously analyses the way in which changes made in the game of Monopoly testify to the secession of the wealthiest. In the original version, the 'Chance' or 'Community Chest' cards required players to pay modest school or hospital fees. Today, it is the taste for luxury that brings rewards or penalties. 'Your museum of modern art brings you a million' or 'Pay 500,000 dollars for your party at Bondi beach in Sydney.' Monopoly shows in its own way the new outrageousness that the wealthy give to the model of a society torn between envy and anger.

A paradoxical phenomenon merits being signalled. If during the twentieth century a process of 'embourgeoisement' of the working class characterized the evolution of industrial society, today we ought to speak of a 'proletarianization' of the rich, from the standpoint of their imaginations. The bourgeois world of the nineteenth century remained haunted by 'pre-modern' values that were essentially derived from the nobility. This is no longer the case. The aspiration of the bourgeoisie to walk in the footsteps of the old aristocracy has disappeared. Today the hyper-rich have dreams that are not qualitatively different from those of the poor. They watch the same football matches and aspire to the same luxury bling. 'The cultural and psychological markers of social position are gradually effaced among the holders of power and wealth.' The aspiration to 'high culture' among the *nouveaux riches* has worn away.[23] Wealth is now sufficient unto itself.

3

The Decline of Empire

Late Antiquity

The last thirty years mark the swing from a world of restraint towards a world of excess. Yesterday, elites 'veiled their successes with old-fashioned decencies'. Now they abandon the middle and working classes to their fates and no longer fear exhibiting their wealth. This rupture can be understood as the passage 'from an age of equipoise to an age of ambition'. These phrases, which ring true as a way of understanding our era, are in fact used by the historian Peter Brown to characterize Late Antiquity and the beginnings of the slow 'decline of the Roman Empire'. The transformations at work at that time indeed very much resemble those we are discussing today.[1] The parallel gives an unsuspected depth to the current upheavals.

Between the reign of Marcus Aurelius (121–180 CE), an emperor fully planted in the ancient world and its values, and that of Constantine (280–337 CE), who was going to open the doors to the Christianization of the world, the Roman Empire profoundly changed its nature. The idea of a general 'crisis' has been mentioned with regard to the third

century, when scholars talk of a 'malaise' of ancient civilization, 'a rise in superstition' or 'the decline of rationalism'.
According to Peter Brown, this malaise is not explained by
material causes (economic decline or growing poverty). For
him, it is the former model of parity among the elites, with
constraints borrowed from the lost past of the ancient pagan
city, that broke down.[2] This crisis corresponded to a collapse
of the equilibrium in the political and social order. He cau-
tions that the transition from the Age of Antonius to the Age
of Constantine was not caused by catastrophic crumbling,
but rather resulted from a shift from one dominant lifestyle
and its forms of expression, to another one, the shift from
an age of equilibrium to an age of ambition.[3]

The old model of parity pushed members of the upper
class to seek honours from the city. 'To lavish funds on
public cults was a way of insuring oneself against envy and
competition. The benefactor gave over wealth to the gods
who, as invisible and immortal, stood for all that could be
shared by the community.'[4] Creating a culture in which men
in strong competition with each other saw themselves constantly called upon to remember what they shared with their
peers and with their local communities was the singular
success of the age of equilibrium.

This model was broken during the third century when
unleashed competition went to work. There was an 'escala-
tion of feuds. We find the cities and provincial aristocracies
in a scramble of competition – city against city in Asia
Minor.'[5] The emperors of the preceding centuries had governed the Empire with a formidable economy of means, by
a 'soft method'. The strong method, a 'militarization' of
social relations, replaced it. What crumbled in the third
century were not the urban aristocracies as such, but rather
the mechanisms by which they had channelled 'their more
disruptive ambitions into their cities and had veiled their
successes in old-fashioned decencies'. The glory of an ancient

city now resided in its private palaces, which dominated the secular city that rose above the temples. Then paganism itself was transformed. Now the Romans would celebrate influential men, the *potentes*, no longer the gods.[6]

Fall of the Western Empire

The decline of Rome has been a constant source of fascination for the moderns, but it is astonishing to learn that this decline was already perceived by the Romans themselves. In the second century, Aelius Aristide marvelled at the splendour of Rome but also inferred that this grandeur had reached its zenith. 'Here is brought from every land and sea all the crops of the seasons and each land, river, lake, as well as of the arts of the Greeks and the Barbarians.' Aristide the Panegyrist ends his oration: 'Whatever one does not see here is not a thing which has existed or does exist.'[7]

However, in this ode to the glory of Rome, a crack is already appearing. The conviction of the dominant classes that their life was bathed in unequalled comfort and material security was also accompanied by a feeling that this state of comfort was devoid of any prospect of subsequent improvement. With Aelius Aristide, the future is mentioned only with the wish that 'the present be prolonged, endless and immutable'.

Many historians today prefer to speak of a long period of transition, running from the third to the seventh centuries, a period during which the traits of the ancient world evolved towards those of the Middle Ages. Yet Aldo Schiavone warns against the hypothesis of continuity. 'By concentrating on the formative processes of the world of late antiquity, and on the inextricable interconnections between old and new that accompanied them, some studies ended up more or less explicitly proposing the idea of a gentle and almost imperceptible transition from the Empire of the second century to the Europe of the early Middle Ages, thereby downplaying, even if unintentionally, the disruptive and catastrophic aspects of the changeover, at least as they were present in Western Europe.'[8] One statistic will convey what signed the death of Rome: demography. The city included about 800,000 inhabitants until 408–10. After the sack by Alaric, it was reduced by half. In the fifth century, the population fell to some 88,000 inhabitants.

Aristide was writing in the middle of the second century, and the first crisis that truly shook Rome occurred in the following one. This is the period that is characterized as the start of Late Antiquity. If you have to choose a line of demarcation when things started to turn downward, it seems indeed to lie in the third century, between the end of the era of Severius (235) and the first part of the regime of Diocletian (284–98).

The haunting problem confronting the Empire related principally to a crisis in public finances, strained by funding a career army; financial deficits were becoming increasingly difficult to solve. In Rome's Golden Age, wars were good value for money. They paid for themselves like an investment, since the colonized regions had to pay taxes that directly filled the public coffers. Wars also allowed Rome to receive cheap products that these same regions – from Spain to Egypt to Syria – had to export to pay their fiscal obligations.

But with time, wars assumed a solely defensive nature. The third century marked the hinge period when the Empire, once conquering and dominant, could no longer manage to hold its borders 'by sole virtue of the dissuasive force of its arms'.[9] Agitation along the frontiers on the Rhine, the Danube and the Euphrates became recurrent. Since the Empire was not in a situation to raise a conscript army to defend the 'fatherland in danger', it had to pay more and more dearly for a professional army. The growing role of

the cavalry necessary to patrol the borders and to intervene rapidly if needed was one example of this financial
burden.

It was also the era when soldier-emperors emerged. The
soft method of the first years of the Empire gave way to a
line of iron-fisted monarchs. Diocletian and Constantine are
the most striking examples. Both would engage in reform of
the tax system and redeploy troops and expenditure.[10]
Thanks to their actions, the crisis was provisionally cur-
tailed, and power re-established. But the wound continued
to bleed. The borders of the Western Empire would become
more and more porous.

A dyke would be broken a little later, in 378, the year of
the defeat of Adrianople during which the Goths and the
Alains routed the Roman armies and killed Emperor Valens
– a battle the writer Alessandro Barbero strikingly por-
trayed.[11] The Barbarians who penetrated the Empire starting
in 375 were seeking status. The Empire resorted to an expe-
dient that would prove fatal: 'to take into its service German
petty kings leading their companies of loyal vassals'.[12] In 375
Emperor Valens had authorized the Goths to settle on the
Roman side of the Danube. The Goths demanded the right
to cross the river to chase away the Huns from Asia who
were threatening them, too. The extinction of Rome is often
dated to the precise year of 476, when the last Western
Roman emperor Romulus Augustulus was deposed. What is
extraordinary is that the dismissal of the last Western
emperor was barely noticed within the Empire!

How the West Became Christian

In the quest for a moral solution to the dissolution of its
civic spirit, Rome would discover and adopt a new religion, Christianity, which did not actually take hold until the
end of the fourth and during the fifth century. Christianity

would plausibly have remained an avant-garde sect without Constantine. As Paul Veyne stresses, the reasons for Constantine's conversion are multiple, but if it had been solely a matter of political calculation, he would not have chosen the religion of only 10 per cent of the Empire, and dismissed the various religions of the 90 per cent. According to Edward Gibbon, the decline of Rome was principally due to the influence of Christianity, which made it lose its 'Roman-ness'.

Christianity would enable Rome to tackle the problem posed by rising social tensions in a different manner. According to Peter Brown, at the moment when 'the model of parity was sapped by the tendency among a few members of the local community to enjoy a privileged status at the expense of their fellows, religious leaders emerged and were encouraged to emerge, in pagan and Christian circles'. Christians would invent a form of 'good neighbourliness' that was much simpler. To say to another person 'I am a Christian' (and to expect to hear back 'Me, too') created comfort. At least in his imagination, the Christian 'did not have to reckon with the high-pitched secular hierarchy of an increasingly pyramidal society alone, over against which there stood in clear outline a spiritual hierarchy of "friends of God"'.[13]

In their quest for God, people of the Church kept their eyes on the earth. They replaced the old philanthropy called 'evergetism', the propensity of the wealthiest Romans to make other citizens benefit from their wealth by organizing banquets and games, with their own charities helping the poor and the sick. But Christianity offered more than consolation over the bitterness of life. It made the course of history seem intelligible, enabling everybody to adjust to its turbulent evolution. Initiation into Christianity freed people from complex earthly identities. According to Paul Veyne in *Comment le monde est devenu Chrétien*, paganism 'left human life as it was, ephemeral and composed of messy

details. Thanks to the Christian God, this life received the
unity of a magnetic field in which each action and each
interior movement assumed a meaning, good or bad. A
woman of the people might thus speak to the Madonna
about her family or conjugal woes. Never would she have
thought of talking about them to Hera or Aphrodite.' For
Veyne, Christianity owed its success to an invention of
genius: 'God's infinite Mercy cares about the fate of humanity, mine and ours [. . .] whereas the pagan gods lived for
themselves.'[14]

This break with pagan religion is similarly stressed by
Jean-Pierre Vernant in (*L'Individu, la mort, l'amour*), who
likewise adopts the intuitions of Louis Dumont on the
sources of individualism.[15] Formerly of course, ancient and
classical Greeks did have an experience of their ego, of their
person, of their body, but this experience was organized differently from ours. For a Greek, *I exist* because I eat and I
run. But I never take my existence through the consciousness
I have of it. 'The world of the individual did not take the
form of a consciousness of self, of an interior universe that
in its radical originality defines the personhood of each.' The
consciousness of self was not yet the apprehension of an 'I'.
The experience of the ego is turned towards the outside, not
the inside. Thus the Cartesian *cogito* has no meaning for a
Greek,[16] who is human only within the city, in the sight of
his peers. As Aristotle said, 'Whosoever is naturally and not
accidentally unfit for society must be either inferior or superior to man.'[17] A Greek in his own eyes is only a mirror that
others offer him.

Jean-Pierre Vernant gives three distinct meanings to what
we call the 'individual' that help us grasp the shift that was
produced during Late Antiquity. (1) Strictly speaking, the
individual measures himself by the room for manoeuvre he
has, his *autonomy* relative to his institutional framework.
(2) As a *subject*, when the individual speaks in his own

name, he enunciates certain traits that make him a singular being. (3) As *ego*, the individual is the ensemble of psychological attitudes and practices that give the subject a dimension of interiority. To simplify an understanding of these three levels, Vernant adds that the individual corresponds to biography, the subject to autobiography and the ego to confessions of the inner life. The first two existed in ancient Greece, but the third would have been unthinkable then.

According to Vernant, the abrupt disappearance of the parity model that made citizens equal to each other, and all men equal in the face of the gods, would create a new form of identity. With the advent of Christianity, the human individual would be defined by 'his most intimate thoughts, his secret imaginings, his nocturnal dreams, his sinful impulses, a constant and obsessive presence in his deep interior'. According to Vernant and Dumont, this is the point of departure for the modern person and individualism. 'With the rise of the holy man, the man of God, a type of individual appears who is going in quest of his true ego, one suspended between the guardian angel who pulls him upward and the demonic forces below that mark the lower boundaries of his personality. Search for God and search for self are two dimensions of the same solitary ordeal.'

Thus the Empire's crisis would conclude with a formidable religious revolution, a new conception of the person, which is the origin of the individualism we know today, that of a being who seeks in an interior self the truth of his personhood. Instead of calling it a soul, Saint Augustine affirms his selfhood: 'This then is my spirit, it is myself. What am I, then, my God?'[18] Christianity gave rise to the modern self-conscious individual. We may ask if a spiritual revolution of the same scope is conceivable today, one provoked by the return of new social tensions, and the difficulty of making intelligible the way the world is moving?

Are We Rome?

Is the decline of the Western Empire again on the horizon? Even Americans are tempted by this parallel.[19] The analogy with Rome obsesses and worries them. In 2007 the Comptroller of the Currency posed the issue in these terms: 'The Roman Republic fell for many reasons, but some of them merit being studied: the decline of moral and political values, a military expansion on foreign territory, the government's budgetary irresponsibility – does that remind you of something? In my opinion, it is time to learn the lessons of history and to take indispensable measures to ensure that the United States remains a foremost power that can resist the work of time.' As the *Financial Times* noted (18 August 2007), 'the question "Are We Rome?" – long a subject of national fascination – has today become another way of asking, "Are We Doomed?" '. Joseph Nye, a Harvard political science professor, added: 'It is true that no other nation since Rome has stayed so high above others, but even Rome ended up crumbling.'

Several interesting resemblances between Rome and America illustrate the scope of this parallel. Cullen Murphy in a book titled precisely *Are We Rome?* notes that in the first place the two powers share a sort of provincialism among their elites. Romans thought (literally) that Rome was the centre of the world. Today, more than 90 per cent of Americans and two-thirds of their state senators do not even have a passport to go abroad! Romans, like Americans, do not owe their strength to a great conqueror like Alexander the Great or William the Conqueror, but to a continuous tendency of the most powerful land to dominate its neighbours, to the point of then considering this domination to be natural. Moreover, both empires tend to claim to be 'the chosen people'.

Americans think the mission to 'democratize' the world that was assigned to them makes them distinct from empires of the past. 'We are a liberating power', George Bush said.[20] As Niall Ferguson (a British historian at Harvard) humorously remarks, within this claim lies the way in which America most resembles past empires, which always saw themselves as the incarnations of civilization in the face of Barbarians. Maybe unwillingly the United States is exporting not only the right to vote and democracy but also everything else along with it: television, the market, divorce, job losses. In short, like all empires in history, it carries in its baggage its own civilization. The parallel offered by Ferguson between the 'civilizers' of the British Empire, Kipling and the rest, and the West's civilizing mission, both of them 'the white man's burden', is totally pertinent.

The second parallel is that the Romans and the Americans fiercely believe in private property. They are pleased ritually to humiliate public figures, but they also maintain an ambivalent love/hate relation with the *nouveaux riches*. The third resemblance, which follows from the preceding one, relates to a privatization of public services. Evergetism, the form of philanthropy described above, is particularly lively in the United States, where the propensity of the wealthiest, such as Bill Gates, Warren Buffett and other billionaires, to create foundations bearing their name is stronger than ever. Even the army does not escape this rampant privatization. The growing difficulties of recruitment obliged the Romans to turn to the Barbarians to fill the ranks of their legions. America is not yet at that stage but is approaching it by hiring private security companies like Blackwater to accompany its troops sent to war zones.

Meanwhile the Europeans like to interpret their own difference from the United States by the measure of a parallel distinction between Rome and Athens. Athens, the cradle of beauty and philosophy, transmitted its culture to Rome, which vulgarized it. Similarly, when Europe was destroyed by its domestic conflicts as Greece once was, it was eventually surpassed by the power of its offshoot, the USA. In both cases, say the Europeans, grace yielded to pragmatism, and beauty ceded to force.

Seen from Europe, the Americans are often presented as 'utilitarian materialists'. To return to our theme, the United States seems the promised land of Homo Economicus, active and entrepreneurial, where the calculation of interest trumps any other consideration. Tocqueville described American materialism in very European terms: 'It is strange to witness the fervent ardour that Americans bring to the pursuit of their well-being and to see how tormented they always seem by a vague fear of not having chosen the shortest way of getting them. An inhabitant of the United States clings to the goods of this world that he seems assured of not dying, yet he is in such haste to grasp the ones that come his way that he seems almost to suffer from perpetual fear of passing away before finding time to enjoy them. [. . .] Death comes at last, catching him before he has tried of this futile pursuit of a complete felicity that remains out of his reach.'[21]

Americans respond that they are 'born free', which has liberated them from European feudalism and from the weight of its monarchical traditions. An anti-government stance is an almost genetic staple of American political philosophy. The state seems to carry the threat of new privileges, of the return to a society founded upon orders inherited from European Old Regimes. For this reason, socialism has never been a popular doctrine in the USA.

However, there is another parallel with Rome that plays a powerful role in the explanation of the American anti-state position: the legacy of slavery. For more than a thousand years of Antiquity, this never produced a serious moral crisis. Even while some slaves were better educated than their masters (holding the roles of secretaries, architects, doctors, policemen and bankers), they remained treated as sub-human.

Its slavery past played a silent and deep role in the United States, too. Trying to explain why Americans manifest such difficulty in embracing the European idea of a welfare state, the scholars Alesina, Glaeser and Sacerdote have shown that the idea that the welfare state is less developed in the USA because Americans are more individualist than Europeans is in fact not a sufficient explanation.[22] The poor do not appear as unfortunates but as radically different 'others' precisely because Americans see social issues through the filter of race. Moreover, each state has a social policy that is always in inverse correlation with the number of blacks who live in that state. To the question 'Why are the poor actually poor?' two-thirds of Americans respond that it is because they are lazy and only a third think that the poor have been unlucky. But the ratio is the reverse as soon as the same question is put to people who have 'recently dined with a black friend'.[23] This is not yet the case with Europeans, a majority of whom continue to think (according to the same poll) that a poor person is someone like others but who did not have any luck.

The election of Obama shows that Americans were victims of an evil they have since tried to cure. In 1950, 50 per cent of whites wished for school segregation! By 1995, that figure had fallen to 4 per cent. In 1963, 61 per cent of Americans were in favour of laws banning interracial marriage. By 1998, they were only 11 per cent. The new tolerance of Americans is a characteristic of the baby-boomers, the generation born after the war. The following generation (Generation X) remains on the same level of tolerance. The traces of slavery remain deep, however, incarnated in a visceral rejection in certain sectors of American society of any form of welfare state. The recent rise of the Tea Party, the political current that wants to dismantle the government and that weighs on the right of the Republican Party, is an illustration. But this current is also the pathological reflection of a new problem in the United States, which is also reminiscent of the moral crisis in the Roman Empire: the decline of civic spirit.

Decline of American Civic Spirit

Individualism is central to the American value system. But it cannot be understood unless it is related to another dimension of their national character that Tocqueville also abundantly stressed: the propensity to form all sorts of communities and associations, secular and religious 'fraternities'. Yet this singular trope started crumbling in the 1960s. Robert Putnam has described this decline in a deep and dense book called *Bowling Alone*,[24] where he tracks the fall of Americans' civic spirit through things like parent-teacher associations (PTAs), bridge clubs and bowling leagues.

In 1964, Americans answered the question 'In general, can you trust other people?' positively at a rate of 77 per cent. In 1960 Daniel Bell and Virginia Held wrote that the participation of Americans in political life had reached its apogee. The famous inauguration speech by John F. Kennedy stood as the standard of a nation that deeply believed in civic involvement: 'My fellow Americans, ask not what your country can do for you, ask what you can do for your country. My fellow citizens of the world, ask not what America will do for you, but what together we can do for the freedom of man.' The feeling of a shared identity and destiny had never been as strong as it was in modern America.

Today, fifty years later, 77 per cent of the Americans questioned declare that their country has lost the sense of community, and that 'selfishness' has become a very serious problem: 'Rather than turning to each other, most people drifted apart, becoming more isolated and wanting to be left alone.'[25] Sixty per cent of baby-boomers (born between 1946 and 1960) believe that. For Generation X (born after 1960), the statistic falls to 50 per cent. Putnam offers a multitude of data testifying to this evolution. The number of those who do not obey a 'stop' sign, for example, has risen from 30 per cent to 90 per cent! Family life becomes more solitary, too. Only a third of households now state that they eat meals together (as opposed to 50 per cent twenty years earlier).

No form of collective life has been spared. The rate of voting in presidential elections has tumbled. If we set aside the southern states, which de facto excluded blacks from the electoral rolls until the civil rights movement of the 1960s, the fall is impressive. The rate of participation reached 85 per cent in 1960, before falling to 50 per cent in 2000. PTAs provide another example of this disengagement. In 1960 – the high point of American civic involvement – one parent in two was a member of a school association. In 2000, the figure slipped below 20 per cent. This decline in civic spirit is all the more surprising because it is concomitant with a rise in education, and citizen engagement tends normally to be stronger among educated persons.

The decline in the labour movement is also analysed by Putnam. Trade unionism assumed importance throughout the first half of the twentieth century. In 1960, 30 per cent of American workers were unionized. This figure had fallen by half in 2000. It is customary to attribute the fall in unionization to the changing nature of the economy. The trend towards the third (or service) sector is less propitious for unions than were the major industries of yesterday. While this transformation obviously plays an important role, it does not explain this tendency within the industrial sector itself. Between 1953 and 1997, the rate of unionization fell there as well, by two-thirds. 'Teamwork stops feeling so amicable when you are subtly competing with your team-mates for your livelihood.'[26] In 1955, 44 per cent of Americans declared that the time spent at work was the most agreeable in their lives. By 1999, only 16 per cent thought so. For a long time the blue-collar workers were the category most affected by economic insecurity. It now touches all labour categories. High-level consultants are in demand, and are handsomely remunerated for their work. But for most of the population, insecurity has had no financial compensation; it remains a cost paid without anything in return.

Nor has religion been spared by this evolution away from civic engagement. American religiosity is a singular characteristic of the country. Still today, almost 90 per cent of Americans believe in God and three-quarters in the immortality of the soul. The corresponding figures in Europe are much lower. But the number of religious 'drop-outs' – those who leave the churches – has almost doubled. And the churches that do arise are not the same kind as those they replace. While the usual Protestant churches were turned towards the world, the new evangelical ones belong to sects that are centred on themselves. Putnam distinguishes two types of social capital. The first, *bridging capital*, is what connects people, giving rise to a community outside one's walls and to meeting others out there. The second, *bonding capital*, is what brings people together, tightens links within the immediate community – but against the rest of the world. It is the second type of social capital that tends to prosper today.

The transformation of American society has been explained in many ways. Increases in female labour and in divorces, which are said to have eroded traditional family values, have been put under the spotlight. The drive of the economy towards the service sector, by eating away union power, is thought to have contributed to destroying the value of labour. But these explanations are feeble, if not mistaken. For example, it is not true that the rise in the number of divorces harms civic involvement. Apart from in houses of worship, those who are divorced are just as present in associations – whether school parents, sports, or politics. Nor is it true that the industrial sector has better resisted the decline in trade unions. The disappearance of the value of labour is a more general phenomenon.

By all accounts, most of the American civic collapse is consistent with one crucial factor: the appearance of the baby-boomers. The generations born after the war undeniably behave differently. They vote much less often than preceding generations; they read fewer newspapers. While two-thirds of those under the age of 35 used to read a newspaper in 1965, half as many did so in 1990. In total, the rate of reading the papers has fallen by 60 per cent, even while education has increased by 60 per cent! And this is not principally tied to the fact that the baby-boomers are getting their news elsewhere, on television, for example. The lowering interest in news is observed on all media. Its place is taken by *infotainment*, which offers a new product situated between information and reality shows.[27]

For Putnam, television plays an essential role in the attitude of baby-boomers. They are the first generation to have been virtually educated thanks to TV. Between 1965 and 1995, an American family earned six more hours of weekly leisure due to the reduction in working time. But this free time was entirely absorbed by time spent in front of a screen: this is now the case with 80 per cent of Americans. Television has 'privatized' any belonging to the public world. The American (naturalized British) poet T. S. Eliot said that television was a 'medium of entertainment which permits millions of people to listen to the same joke at the same time, and yet remain lonesome'.[28] A Canadian study has enabled comparison between the behaviour of two regions that got access to television within a few years of each other (for technical reasons). It shows that the region that received it first lost several points in civic participation in comparison to the other.

Yet it would be ridiculous to impute the spurt in individualism observed in the United States to television alone. The revolt of May 1968, one of the most visible manifestations of the change in generations, was observed in all advanced countries, from Paris to Berkeley, and bears the trace of many other mutations. Member of the European Parliament Henri Weber, analysing its roots throughout the industrialized world, argues that the revolt was harshest in Germany and Japan, two countries where the conflict of baby-boomers with their parents was most intense, which for him attests to a more general refusal of parental authority. Whatever the cause, the baby-boomers are at the origin of a decisive swerve, of a 'cultural revolution' in relation to society. More tolerant on the one hand, they have also become more individualistic.

New forms of communities have certainly appeared: on the left, Greenpeace, the ecological organization, and on the right, the Pro-Life movement against abortion. But the volatility of their members is very high. Most people are content to sign a cheque. When the directors of Greenpeace decided to reduce their e-mail solicitations, their membership dropped by 85 per cent. A good number of self-help groups have also arisen, but they do not have the same function as those they replaced. To participate in Alcoholics Anonymous does not lead to any form of traditional civic involvement, whether simply going to vote or volunteering for charity work. These are 'utilitarian' groups 'that provide occasions for individuals to focus on themselves in the presence of others'.[29]

American Exceptionalism

There does exist one real difference between Rome and America that recent evolutions do not modify. The Romans were not curious! With regard to innovation, they were clearly inferior to the Chinese, their contemporaries. Over the same period, the Han Dynasty went much further. The Chinese discovered the compass, the body's daily rhythms, the hexagonal structure of snowflakes . . . They understood the principle of crop rotation and irrigation techniques; in mathematics, they used negative numbers and discovered decimal fractions. The Romans did build endless roads and majestic aqueducts, they discovered cement and perhaps the siphon. They invented the watermill, but perfecting and diffusing it were very slow. The most widespread machines in the Roman Empire were operated by animals and slaves, and both of them experienced hell on earth.

The attitude in America in the face of machines and innovations is totally different. In an almost obsessive way, Americans rush after innovations, holding that the new is almost by definition superior to the old. American heroes were Thomas Edison yesterday, and Steve Jobs today. According to Vaclav Smil, 'the average American has machines whose capacity may be estimated to be a million times higher than those of a Roman'.[30]

This insatiable quest for innovation has several sources. The consumer is himself one of the principal motor forces, since consumers are immediately sensitive to novelties of all kinds. As Tocqueville said, a consumer is 'hasty to grasp all that comes within his reach'. Another reason is well known by economic historians. The United States has long remained a land where labour was a rare resource, the colonists having exterminated the natives, who were not very numerous to begin with. Quickly (starting in the early nineteenth century), salaries grew above European levels, which would be the cause of great waves of transatlantic migration. According to the theory of H. J. Habakkuk, taken up by the growth theorist Paul Romer, this situation led to the constant search for techniques aiming to economize on the labour factor. This was one of the major springboards of American economic growth.

Another explanation, valid starting with the Second World War, relates to the role of the Defense Department. The

United States does not have an 'industrial policy' in the sense that this is understood in Europe (the policy that engendered the Airbus) or in Japan (where the role of the famous MITI has been long observed), but it does possess a key actor: the DOD. The United States spends more on defence than the fifteen next countries combined. Therefore the success of Boeing owes much to Pentagon expenditure: the Boeing 707 is almost identical to the Air Force supply aircraft KC135, with portholes added. The transistor was invented at Bell Laboratories, the jewel of AT&T and a great beneficiary of military subsidies. With regard to innovation, the role of DARPA (Defense Advanced Research Projects Agency) is essential. Between 1955 and 1985, military expenditure in the United States represented on average 7.5 per cent of American GDP.[31]

In June 2002, George W. Bush asserted that America had and intended to keep uncontested military supremacy, making any attempt at an arms race totally absurd. Will America's technological strength allow it to avoid the retreat of the Romans in the face of the invading Barbarians? No doubt, as long as the Americans keep the monopoly on cutting-edge technology. However, here one could make another parallel with Rome. Then, the Barbarians had gradually joined the legions, since there weren't enough Roman candidates. Now, it is not Barbarian generals who are leading armies, but hordes of Asian students who come to study in American universities. More than half the doctoral theses defended in science and engineering are written by students born outside the country. The progressive laziness of the Romans, which led them to subcontract the conduct of war to these Barbarians, has its parallel in the low interest native-born Americans manifest in scientific disciplines. The professions of law and finance attract many more of America's gilded youth than do the hard sciences like physics or mathematics.

The Institute of International Education reveals that 723,000 foreign students frequented American campuses in 2010–2011 (bringing almost 20 million dollars to the institutions that admit them).[32] This is triple the total reached at the start of the 1980s. Half of these foreign students are studying science. 'In certain disciplines that have been deserted by young Americans, like the life sciences or engineering, Asians form the majority in the labs, and this omnipresence leaps out to be noticed by all visitors.'[33]

Comparisons between Rome and Washington, however, do reach their limits. The Asian students who come to the United States often stay there and become good Americans. And when they go home, they try much more to create an international scientific community than to be the rear-guard of a Barbarian invasion. This analogy carries the germ of the fundamental question that the twenty-first century will have to answer. Will globalization (economic and technological) be a factor for peace by diffusing common values? Or on the contrary, by creating a multipolar world, will it sharpen the old quarrels that more than once led the European countries to tip into war?

4

De-Centring the World

From New York to Shanghai

The second half of the twentieth century was inhabited by the idea of a death struggle between Moscow and Washington, 'the modern equivalent of the conflict between Sparta and Athens'. America won and its partisans were able to see that victory as Athens' revenge on Sparta. The most surprising thing is the speed with which the Cold War was forgotten. In a few months, 'this great conflict collapsed all by itself and the Cold War seemed as old-fashioned as the Thirty Years War'. As Aldo Schiavone writes in *Histoire et destin*, the world of yesterday has disappeared in a 'flapping of wings, entrained by a wave of global capitalist innovation: finance, communication, globalization'.[1]

The growth of emerging countries has cost the West its monopoly on modernity. The skyscrapers are now higher in Shanghai than in New York. Las Vegas has been outstripped by Macao. The foreign traveller who comes to visit New York is struck by a feeling of 'old modernity', that of the Chrysler Building or Coca-Cola bottles. As Gertrude Stein said, 'America is the oldest country because we have been modern for so long.'[2]

World growth testifies to the striking upheaval. At the start of the 1990s, it was split between 70 per cent in the rich countries and 30 per cent in the poor countries. Symbolically, in 2001 the two curves intersected at half-and-half. Since then, the proportions have exactly inverted. World growth now belongs 70 per cent to the emerging countries; the number of them whose growth rate has reached or surpassed double that of Western countries has risen from 12 in the 1990s to 65 in the 2000s.[3]

If we consider the level of wealth (rather than growth rate), these evolutions are much slower but just as remarkable. In 1990, the distribution of world wealth was the following: 60 per cent belonged to the richest countries and 40 per cent to the poorest. In 2030, it will be the reverse: 40 per cent will belong to the rich and 60 per cent to the poor. A pendulum swing is visible across the world. A new internal sea, the Pacific, becomes the *mare nostrum* of the new capitalism, after the Mediterranean in antiquity and then the Atlantic in the modern age.

Put into perspective, these deformations are not astonishing. In fact, they can be interpreted as a return to a just balance. In 1820, the 'emerging' countries represented two-thirds of the world's wealth. In a century, their share collapsed. China, for example, went down from 40 per cent to five per cent of total wealth between 1800 and 1900! The explanation is simple: in the eighteenth century, the weight of populations essentially fixed the share that countries took in world wealth. The more populous a region, the richer it was, for the simple reason that the revenue per inhabitant was almost identical from one land to another. The nineteenth century upset this correlation. With the Industrial Revolution of the eighteenth century, the populated lands of Europe could raise themselves very much above their demographic situation. Thus England dominated the world with less than two per cent of the world population.

Starting in the nineteenth century (but the roots go back to the sixteenth century), the human species split. The great civilizations of the past, which were almost on a par with each other, were all surpassed by the West – although nothing in the year 1000 would have presaged that it would be ascendant over the others. Commenting on the decline of Islam or that of China, specialists like Lewis Mumford or David Landes explain that each of these civilizations that were once brilliant slumped into political and religious conservatism, which prevented them from absorbing the kinds of progress realized in the great strides taken by the West in this period.

In the twenty-first century, with the more rapid diffusion of technologies, the weight of population began again to exert its law on the equilibrium of world wealth. The poor countries, which had long known more vigorous demographics, were ready to accumulate population and wealth concurrently. This scenario had already occurred in Europe. Germany was a backward country at the start of the nineteenth century. By the dawn of the twentieth century, it had become the most populated and the richest, having its revenge on the France that had once humiliated it.

In turn the emergent countries are now following the schema borrowed from the West and Japan: the path leading rural societies to industrialize, to urbanize and to be educated according to a sequence that the economist Walt Rostow had called in the 1960s a series of 'stages' of economic growth. Those like Huntington who interpret the world as a clash of civilizations seem to ignore how porous cultural barriers are. The spectacular divergence of the postwar destinies of Taiwan and the People's Republic of China illustrates this permeability. Their 'Sino-ness' has had much less influence on the lifestyle of these two 'regions' than the openness of one and the closure of the other to commerce and ideas.

The question of demographics, no doubt the most important in human history, shows the parallel between these processes. The emerging countries, whatever their geographic zone and religion, are engaged in a transition that makes the number of infants per woman fall from seven or more, the birth-rate characterizing pre-industrial societies) to levels that tend on average towards those of rich countries, beyond the threshold of reproduction of 2.1 infants per woman. Everywhere in the world a single strategy for growth seems to be required.

Rethinking Poverty

Looking at the impressive growth figures of emerging countries, it is easy to forget the immense destitution that the peoples of the planet suffer. Half of humans live on less than two euros a day. The enrichment of the south is an indisputable fact, but this is an average. Even in cases that are *a priori* most favourable, the situation is distressing. If the east coast of China has become the new workshop of the world, 800 million poor peasants remain waiting for the right to come and live there. India is a country where more than half the population still does not know how to read and write. The new urban middle class in India may have reached perhaps 300 million people. But they live alongside 700 million villagers stuck in poverty. Peasants who kill themselves because they cannot pay their debts have never been so numerous. Between 1997 and 2008, almost 200,000 ruined Indian farmers committed suicide. The old cycle of debt, usury and dependency continues to strike the most vulnerable.

The task awaiting the poor countries in order to become in turn centres of prosperity remains considerable – and for many of them the prospect is daunting. To hope to become fully-fledged actors in globalization they have – sometimes starting with nothing – to educate and care for their peoples, and to master technologies in constant evolution. For most of the poor people of our planet, globalization remains a fleeting mirage.

To understand poverty today does not mean understanding another race, that of the poor, but understanding how the human species struggles when it is deprived of all the goods that have become ordinary in rich countries. Abijit Banerjee and Esther Duflo have offered a staggering study that goes much further than previous research.[4] While some economists are tempted to see in poverty a failure of the poor themselves, they show that it reveals human rationality when deprived of the support of competent and legitimate institutions to help people to decide what to do.

Several examples illustrate these misunderstandings. Each year, nine million children die before their fifth birthday. Diarrhoea is a major cause of this mortality. It might be contained by resorting to chlorine, which does not cost very much. Why is it not used more? Malaria causes the death of a million persons each year, most of them African children. Sleeping under a mosquito net treated with insecticide could reduce the incidence of this disease by half. A mosquito net costs only about ten euros. Again, why are they not more used? Agriculture is the main sector of activity of the poor. The fertilizers that would enable raising agricultural productivity are clearly under-utilized. Here again, why are they not more widespread?

Two theories – one might say two ideologies – have long been confronting each other over the answer to these questions. The first is the 'Victorian' theory of poverty, named after Queen Victoria, under whose reign the idea was developed. People are poor because they are indigent. It is vain to try to encourage them to do what is good for them: they are poor precisely because they do not want what is good for them. At the other pole, the 'progressive' theory argues exactly the contrary. It is poverty itself that is responsible for the indigence of those who suffer from it. It is not because they are different that the poor fail. They are subject to the same difficulties, but do not possess the resources that would enable them to face them. A great 'Marshall Plan' could eradicate poverty.[5]

The problem that Banerjee and Duflo point out is that, yes, the poor do not possess an adequate framework for acting effectively, but that, no, the resources that are lacking are not just financial. In a rich country, a household does not ask about whether to vaccinate or educate its children, to set aside money for retirement, or know that you have to take out home and car insurance. Almost everything is taken charge of by society, and in the West the state is the memory of history. It is social institutions like those for health, education and social security that decide that you have to vaccinate children and educate them.

The inhabitant of a poor country must bear everything himself, and the burden often crushes him – or her. He would like to invest in fertilizer, for example, but the time is too long between the harvest and the next planting. When one offers farmers the chance to buy coupons after the harvest to pre-pay for fertilizer for the next planting, then they do so immediately. But saving is very complicated when secure financial instruments are lacking, when the pressure of current needs is constant. Not that the poor are especially more indigent than the inhabitants of rich countries. The credit cards that ruined America show that the temptation to over-consume is very strong there, too. The poor like the rich need institutional support to manage their life cycles rationally. Moreover, according to Esther Duflo,[6] the success of micro-credit relates undoubtedly to the fact that it functions like Alcoholics Anonymous in that it puts borrowers under close surveillance. Similarly, according to the work of Pascaline Dupas, the poor will use mosquito nets against malaria, but not without time spent learning how, and after verifying that they are truly effective.

The poor spend a lot of money to maintain their human capital, especially taking care of their health, which sometimes absorbs a considerable share of their revenue. Still, it is very difficult to pay for preventive measures when meagre resources are constantly required for other needs. Like sugared tea, an old television set in poor repair gives a pleasure that trumps any investment whose return is uncertain and deferred. Quite simply, the poor are also looking for happiness.

In any case, a lesson leaps out from these studies: the cultural explanations of poverty seem quite removed from the reality. In effect, the poor person is a rich one left to fend for him or herself, without the support of institutions that help the person to take 'good' decisions. As proof, when the opportunities are presented, as is the case in Asia today, they are seized immediately.

Asia Takes off Badly

'Modernization' has long haunted the countries of the South. In the 1950s and 1960s, the developing countries that are today called emerging believed often that their time had come, and each time the disappointment was cruel. Former French President General de Gaulle had a killer phrase: 'Brazil is a country of the future that will long remain so.' In fact, while the phases of acceleration of growth were legion in the postwar years, the phases of collapse were just as many. In the course of the last sixty years, Ricardo Haussmann and his co-authors have counted 83 'false starts'.[7]

After the war, Asia itself had taken off badly. Japan had been broken by two atomic bombs. India was cut in two after independence. China exited from the world game to undergo a Maoist cure. Asia as a whole knew growth that was well below its potential. India grew at two per cent in the 1950s, but stumbled and stagnated at a low-water mark twice below the start of the 1960s. Thanks to medical progress, cholera, malaria and smallpox retreated and life expectancy was extended spectacularly in India, from 32 to 51 years. But this improvement remained without any great impact on education, for example. Between 1955 and 1965, Indonesia stagnated, like Malaysia and Singapore.

From the end of the 1960s, in the face of all these failures, Western economists gradually backed the idea that Asia was suffering from 'cultural handicaps' that made it impossible for it to follow a path to sustained growth. Gunnar Myrdal, a famous Swedish economist who was a specialist in poverty, devoted three volumes to Asian economies. His conclusion was categorical: India would never manage to sustain durable economic growth because it was dominated by an Asian culture too removed from the materialist ('acquisitive') culture that inhabits the West.[8] This judgement proved to be rather hasty.

Only Japan created surprise by defying the supposed cultural determinism of the rest of Asia. In the course of the 1960s, the Japanese economy passed from peripheral status to a central role. In three decades, Japanese revenue multiplied by four! At a forced march, Japan absorbed one industry after another: photo cameras, sewing machines, shipbuilding, then automobiles and steel making. Books describing the Japanese ascent multiplied (e.g. *Japan as Number One, Why has Japan Succeeded?*). A joke of that period recounts that an American on death row wanted to die before his Japanese sidekick so as not to suffer another lesson on Japanese management! However, commenting on the Japanese success back in 1984, the great economist Morishima[9] gave a culturalist reason, explaining learnedly why it could never be repeated in China: for him, Japanese success relates to the fact that they are not Confucians, like the Chinese, but believe in Shintoism, the equivalent of Protestantism in Asia . . . an analysis that would also be soon belied by the facts.

The new growth over all of Asia today shows in fact how fragile these explanations were. Despite handicaps that appeared insurmountable, the continent has bluntly testified to an economic vitality that was unthinkable a few years earlier. Economists, although they are gradually accepting historical factors and mentalities among the determinants of growth, were caught off-guard. In 1993, the World Bank published 'The East Asian Miracle: Economic Growth and Economic Policy' and its explanation of the miracle is simple.[10] Everything happens suddenly just like in the economics books that people had recently been burning: savings, education and openness to world trade are indeed factors of growth. An autocatalytic phenomenon occurs. Japanese success went on to inspire the 'four dragons': South Korea, Singapore, Taiwan and Hong Kong. Then their successes mobilized the Chinese. The Chinese reforms awakened the Indians. Like a fire that sets a dry prairie ablaze, capitalism converted Asia. Homo Economicus gallantly invited himself. And no tradition or superstition has prevented him from staying there.

On China

Beneath the tornado of this world in transition, a major shift is now clear: the new Chinese power. In certain respects, the conflict between Athens and Sparta has recommenced in a different guise. China has become a threat. Erik Izraelewicz,[11] after having written a first book titled *Quand la Chine change le monde* (*When China Changes the World*, 2005) published a second whose title, *L'Arrogance Chinoise* (*Chinese Arrogance*, 2011), signalled the new view among Westerners. 'Five years ago, all the major figures of Chinese industry courted their Western homologues in the hope of a hypothetical marriage. Today the same industrialists disdain those colleagues, when they do not try to import them. No sector has been spared: automobiles, aeronautics, nuclear energy.' There are many examples to illustrate the Chinese success. Silicon Valley, for example, now buys half of its solar panels in China. In four years the Chinese high-speed train has become an export product that seduces Saudi Arabia, South Africa and California.

The economic weight of China gradually tends to reflect that of its population. The huge country directly accounts for 20 per cent of the world population, for (only) 10 per cent of the wealth, 30 per cent of world growth.[12] Every Chinese statistic oscillates between these figures. Thus China accounts for 15 per cent of Internet users, 20 per cent of CO_2 emissions and exchange reserves, 27 per cent of the number of smokers in the world, 29 per cent of the consumption of luxury products and 40 per cent of steel production. At a stupefying speed, China has erased two centuries of economic stagnation. Journalist Fareed Zakaria, like all observers who have had the same experience, describes the swiftness of transformations: 'Fifteen years ago, when I first went to Shanghai, Pudong in the east of the city was undeveloped countryside. Today it is the city's financial district, densely studded with towers of glass and steel and lit like a Christmas tree every night. It is eight times the size of London's new financial district, Canary Wharf.'[13]

The Chinese already are exhibiting the most characteristic (and caricatured) traits of the contemporary world: real estate speculation, automobile consumption, and mass tourism (40 million Chinese tourists patrol the world). China includes the greatest number of Web surfers on the planet, about 750 million of them. Google has had to send its Asian activities to Hong Kong, and Facebook has had to enhance its privacy protection standards. But Baidu, a Chinese computer search engine created in 2000, is utilized by 70 per cent of the Internet users there. China Mobile has 560 million subscribers, while Vodafone has 'only' 350 million.

China in forty years has passed from Mao's Cultural Revolution to a capitalist one. It has become a country where unprecedented disparities prevail. Vuitton and Gucci buildings spring out of the ground in the posh districts of Shanghai, Canton or Shenzhen. 'Chinese consumers who can afford international name brands already number 250 million' (13 per cent of the total Chinese population). But at the same time, at the other end of the spectrum, the writer Hu Yua, author of the magnificent novel *Brothers*, recounts a new item about a couple who argued because they could not give their child a banana. An overwhelmed husband committed suicide, despairing about being a good-for-nothing, and then the wife hanged herself.[14]

Behind the 'Chinese miracle' we find a condensation of the novels of Dickens and of Balzac, tales of the new poor and the new bourgeoisie. Ecological disasters affect the lives of 560 million city dwellers, of which only 1 per cent breathe air that is considered healthy by the standards of the European Union. Nine thousand chemical factories cause unbearable pollution more than the mines of Yang Tse alone. More than a quarter of Chinese rivers are 'so polluted that they have lost the capacity to fulfil their ecological function'. In the health domain, a sick person who goes into hospital is first interrogated about his financial resources. This type of anecdote, which we are accustomed to hearing about the United States, is frequently heard today in China.

'The secret of the world's factory is all these migrant workers who come from the countryside and represent very low labour costs', according to the sociologist Lu Huilin, quoted in *Le Monde*.[15] Everywhere else in the world, workers live, create families and consume. But in the case of China, their movement to the city is transitory because they have to return to their mother's commune if they want to take advantage of public services (school, hospital, etc.).

Things are changing, under pressure from manpower needs, but the Chinese paradox remains: the second largest economic power in the world, having outstripped Japan in the summer of 2010, is a power that is actually poor, in one-hundredth place in the UN's index of human development. Inequalities attain totally unprecedented levels in a country that fifty years ago still lived under an ultra-egalitarian Maoist regime. Yu Hua, a vigilant scrutinizer of the Chinese situation, describes a programme on Chinese television where humble people are asked about their dreams. A boy from Peking answered that he wanted a Boeing (a real one, not a toy). The other child, a little girl from the northwest of the country, answered that she wanted a pair of sneakers. Yu Hua adds that the pair of sneakers is no doubt more inaccessible for the little girl than the Boeing for the little Peking boy.

Good-Bye Lenin

The Chinese case offers specialists in the theory of happiness an incomparable 'natural experiment'. In less than three decades, 300 million Chinese have risen from poverty (defined by the threshold of a dollar a day). The average income has increased four-fold! It is as if a French person earning 1,500 euros a week in 1990 found himself earning 6,000 euros in 2010. If money makes happiness, even in a partial or ephemeral way, the result should be spectacular. But it is nothing of the sort, and the Chinese remain on average at their initial level. The upper third of the population does see its happiness increase, but the lower third loses by the same proportions. The median third, even though they take part in the general rise in income, stagnates.[16] The fallout from growth explains this lag.

China is following a trajectory very close to that experienced by the former countries of Eastern Europe: loss of job security, the gradual bankruptcy of traditional public enterprises and rising unemployment have become the new way of living. In general, the inhabitants of the former East Germany are satisfied with the way their material conditions have been evolving, but their disappointments concerning jobs, health and nursery crèches spoil the feast.[17] In the end, they have not recorded a rise in their indices of satisfaction, either. Nobody in China seriously thinks of going backward, towards Maoism. But that regime is today the subject of a newfound nostalgia: 85 per cent of those surveyed by Internet think 'it would be a good thing' if Mao were re-awakened today.

The French sociologist Emile Durkheim used the term 'anomie' to characterize a social state where the old norms have disappeared, while the new ones delay their appearance. People no longer know what to expect from others, or what kind of reciprocity they can count on . . . Urban China is revisiting exactly the same situation as described by Durkheim in France at the end of the nineteenth century. The British economist John Knight has analysed this process in a very direct way. According to his estimations, in China urban happiness is a function of everybody's distance from the upper quarter of the population. Therefore frustration is constant for 75 per cent of city-dwellers. Inversely, in rural China 70 per cent of people compare themselves to other villagers whose income is close to their own. The enrichment of some is interpreted as the promise of enrichment for the rest.[18] Ultimately the cities, although three times richer than the countryside, are less happy! What has disappeared in the towns is the feeling of a shared community, which still binds together the inhabitants of villages. In the cities, rivalry has taken the upper hand, effacing the benefits of a material prosperity that is nevertheless much higher.

Moreover, the Chinese conserve certain stubborn archaisms that modernization has not caused to disappear. They prefer boys to girls. The single child policy has produced an abysmal deficit of girls, creating sharp competition on the matrimonial market. The ultra-sound technique that allows parents to determine in advance the sex of their baby has had a determining influence. In 1980, the sex ratio was 1.07 boys to girls. By 2007, it had moved to 1.22. A good fifth of girls in relation to boys are missing. The number of surplus men aged over twenty rose above 32 million in 2005, more than the total masculine population of Italy or Canada. China was not the only country to experience such an evolution: we also observe it to a lesser extent in Korea, India, Vietnam, Singapore, Taiwan and Hong Kong. The disequilibrium produced by these 'missing women', to use the title of an article by Amartya Sen,[19] provokes a rise in violence. Robert Muchenbled in his book *A History of Violence*[20] shows that it is frequently due to young men, and is sharper if matrimonial competition is keen. According to studies that have tried to quantify this phenomenon, to shift from 1.10 merely to 1.11 boys per girl would increase criminality by 3 per cent. In China, this would mean that one-seventh of its violence would be explained by this mechanism alone!

The single child policy produces many other pathologies. The only son is a 'little emperor'. He is an only child living with two parents and four grandparents. The parents' whole strategy aims to ensure him as lofty a destiny as possible, and above all to provide a wife for him. To establish their son's status, parents ruin themselves with ostentatious expenditure above their means. According to the economist Zhang Xiaobo,[21] poor people devote considerable sums to community expenses like funerals, marriages, family parties. Zhang Xiaobo and his co-authors show that in rural China these expenses oblige villagers to curtail drastically their basic household expenditure. Obviously there is nothing new under the sun; anthropologists have studied these rites (notably Mauss's work on the potlatch) in detail. The Chinese paradox is that these practices seem to have become more widespread when related to wealth levels, which are also rising sharply. In the villages studied, the share of food consumption dropped from 48 to 42 per cent between 2005 and 2009. Meanwhile, the share of gifts to the community rose from 8 to 17 per cent. China is subject to a form of suffering that is dictated by the disequilibria that the country has imposed on itself: the search for fiancées for its sons.

Zhang Xiaobo considers that this disparity relates to a significant cause of Chinese economic success: households work and save more when they have a son! More than 20 per cent of economic growth might be attributed to this phenomenon. He notes that this pertains less to regions where the status of women is better (for example, areas that produce tea, which is cultivated by women). At the heart of Chinese growth, we find an outpouring of other 'archaic' passions that endure, even if they are not exacerbated. Homo Economicus may get considerably richer, as he does in China today. It remains to be seen if this suffices to make humans feel the 'foretaste of happiness and peace' . . .

Democracy and Capitalism

No question is more important for the future of the world than whether China (as it gets richer) will become in its turn a democracy. In 1989, the year when the Berlin Wall fell, another equally important event occurred: the demonstrations in Tiananmen Square were bloodily crushed. The ordinary Chinese understood abruptly that political passions would not be tolerated. 'Political passions that had accumulated since the Cultural Revolution had finally expended themselves completely in one fell swoop, to be replaced by a passion for getting rich. When everyone united in the urge to make money, the economic surge of the 1990s was the natural outcome.' With humour, Yu Hua recounts how the country passed from the cult of Chairman Mao, the supreme leader, to the cult of 'fashion leaders and elegance leaders, leaders in charm. [. . .] So intense is the competition and so unbearable the pressure that, for many Chinese, survival is like war itself.'[22]

'Some Western intellectuals take the view that an economy can enjoy rapid growth only in a society where the political system is fully democratic. They find it astonishing that in a nation where politics is far from transparent, the economy can develop at such an impressive pace.'[23] For Yu Hua this 'energy' is what the Cultural Revolution released. Violence against persons remains the same; only the manner has changed. Mao Zedong had a phrase that young students learned by heart: 'The Revolution is not a dinner party [. . .] It is an insurrection, an act of violence.' It is the same violence that today explains the desire to get rich.

For a Westerner the Chinese mystery is how a despotic regime can avoid falling into nepotism and corruption. The answer is that China swings between these two evils. They call 'young princes' those sons of Chinese leaders who take the places of their elders. Corruption scandals appear regularly on the front pages of the Chinese press. The international press echoed this at the start of 2012 with the disgrace of one of the highest party leaders, Bo Xilai, himself the 'red prince' whose wife, Gu Kailai, was accused of the murder of one of his British associates who was apparently trying to blackmail him.

Yu Hua inverts the ritual question of the link between democracy and prosperity in an ironic and cruel way. According to him, it is the *lack* of democracy that has enabled the staggering development of the economy! Violent expulsions of residents enable the government to raze property destined to become industrial wasteland. Repression of the working class limits salaries. On 13 November 2009, a resident of Chengdu called Tang Fuzhen threw Molotov cocktails at those who had come to demolish her house, before she set herself on fire. This affair moved public opinion. Five law professors from the University of Peking argued that the Constitution had been infringed by the expulsion. But one month later, on 16 December 2009, another woman, coming home after doing her errands, found her house razed to the ground.[24]

Anatole Kaletsky speaks of 'Capitalism 4.0' to character-ize 'an authoritarian capitalism conducted by the state and inspired by Asiatic values'.[25] Lee Kwan Yew, the grand master of Singapore, has made himself the champion of an 'Asiatic authoritarianism' that despises the individualist and libertar-ian values of the West; he argues that the Asiatic model is both more efficient and more just.[26] In an essential book titled *Development as Freedom*, Amartya Sen ripostes that 'Aung San Suu Kyi has no less legitimacy – indeed clearly has rather more – in interpreting what the Burmese want than have the military rulers of Myanmar.' He adds, 'It is by no means clear to me that Confucius in this respect is more authoritarian than Augustine or Plato.'[27] To think of freedom as a Western attribute reflects the nasty habit of judging the past by the present, of forgetting the Inquisition and the tragedies of the twentieth century.

For Sen, development ought to lead to increasing the range of possibilities for everyone. Freedom of opinion is an inte-gral part of development. Democracy obeys a different logic from that of prosperity. India since independence has imported the parliamentary institutions of the United Kingdom and has become an irreproachable democracy (except for the three years when Indira Ghandi suspended democratic institutions at the end of the 1970s). Botswana is another country that shows it is possible for a poor country to become an irreproachable democracy. When the country became independent from Great Britain in 1965, it had only 22 people who had attended university and 100 who had attended high school. But Botswana inherited a society at peace with itself, essentially because the British had found nothing truly interesting to do there! By contrast, many oil monarchies, although infinitely richer, remain non-democratic, and the major recent advance in Saudi Arabia was to allow women to drive a car without their husbands! Wealth thus seems neither necessary nor sufficient to guarantee the passage to democracy.

The Arab Spring has offered a new episode in the democratic aspiration of peoples that had been quickly condemned to despotism. Several writers have spoken of an 'Arab exception', pushing back in time (to the seventeenth century) the great bifurcation between Islam and the West. This was what Bernard Lewis did in his controversial book *What Went Wrong*; however, he neglected to note that the same scenario was produced in China in the same era. Now the issue has been posed again. Why have Arab countries missed the turn taken by other countries towards democracy and/ or growth; why has radical Islamism arisen as the (only) alternative to the dictatorships now in place?

Ishac Diwan has proposed a fascinating explanation of this enigma.[28] When the Soviet Union dissolved, its model of a planned economy, which had inspired a good number of countries such as India under the Nehrus or the Turkey of Ataturk, was likewise interred. In 1991, the Indian elections gave power to the government of P. V. Narasimha Rao, elected on a reform programme and on economic openness. 1990 was also the year when Nelson Mandela was freed. Without being the 'end of History', 1989 certainly marks the end of the world as it had been known since the Bolshevik Revolution.

In the Arab case, the crumbling of the USSR also undermined its economic model, but this aroused radical Islamists rather than the liberal elite who were spokesmen of the democratic aspiration. This bifurcation relates to several elements. According to Diwan, in the first place there is growing corruption of the political elites who 'liberalize' the economy solely for their profit. The spouses, brothers-in-law and sons of Gaddafi and Ben Ali and Mubarak all entered unhesitatingly into the arena of corruption. The voracity of their kin made the autocrats lose any sense of political perspective. September 11th 2001 had a powerful and paradoxical effect. Knowing they were supported by the West in the eradication of Islamism, the Arab dictatorships gave free rein to their cupidity. The growing repression then played a dialectic role of legitimation. By hardening their regimes, they gained in legitimacy in the West, along the way strengthening the Islamism that served as their screen. In Egypt as in Tunisia, it was paradoxically the prospect of new elections that ignited the powder keg: Ben Ali wanted a fifth term in Tunisia, and Mubarak a sixth term in Egypt. The masquerade of new and rigged elections was experienced as a provocation, which sharpened people's frustrations and pushed them to revolution.

Homo Politicus

Crises rarely remain confined to the economic sphere. They can overthrow tyrants. Nobody doubts that the Ben Alis and Mubaraks should have been sacked after the crisis that began in 2008. The philosopher Karl Popper once gave this minimal definition of democracy: to allow people to overthrow bad leaders without violence. But history shows that crises may also put weak democracies in peril, like the Weimar Republic in the 1930s. However, the question posed in the Chinese case is symmetrical. Does prosperity contain the possible ferment for democratic aspirations? The *Wall Street Journal* devoted a major debate to this complex question in 2007.

This exchange was called the 'new Cambridge Controversy' since it pitted Edward Glaeser against Daron Acemoglu, both professors in Cambridge, across the river from Boston, the former at Harvard, the latter at MIT. The radically opposed views of these two eminent professors illuminated the ambiguity of the topic.

Glaeser was convinced that economic development leads to democracy for a fundamental reason: growth requires educating the population, and education necessarily leads to democracy. According to him, education is in effect an infallible lever of democracy: 95 per cent of 'educated' democracies in 1960 remained so in the course of the following forty years. Inversely, only 50 per cent of democracies that are badly or mediocrely educated remain so, tipping over into dictatorship in less than a decade on average. But on the other hand, Glaeser is much more sceptical about the propensity of democracies to sustain economic growth. For him, no data prove that democracy lifts growth. Some studies show that democracy may even *reduce* growth – when it unleashes populist one-upmanship among parties, for example.[29] Obviously dictatorships may produce their own economic catastrophes. The Mobutus and Kim Jongs of the planet enrich their courtiers and starve their peoples. But Singapore under Lee Kwan Yew, South Korea under Park Chung Hee, or China today show that dictatorships may also perfectly favour economic development.

For his part, Acemoglu thinks exactly the opposite! Of course the richest countries are on average more educated, more tolerant and more democratic. But the causality is not clear. He recalls the case of Germany: the foremost industrial nation of Europe, certainly one of the most educated, toppled into Nazism. It was military defeat that would durably establish German parliamentary democracy, as in Japan, not wealth or education. Nothing proves that countries that educate themselves tend to become more democratic. The ex-USSR and Cuba attained high levels of education. But Cuba is still not democratic, and Russian democracy remains quite superficial. Acemoglu adds that students demonstrate, today like yesterday, against the government in power, but not necessarily in favour of democracy. In 1917 they supported Lenin, in 1968 they supported Mao, in 1979 they supported Ayatollah Khomeini. Students are always a threat to current regimes, and they serve as a 'reality test' in the face of crises.

In contrast to Glaeser, Acemoglu still thinks that democracy is indeed a factor for growth, at least in the very long term. Economic growth requires innovation and technological progress, which constantly pose a challenge to the advantages that have been acquired. Democracy offers a better playing field since it reduces privileges and unearned income. A dictatorial regime tends to protect the interests of influential groups, which in the long term become factors of blockage. On a long timescale, according to Acemoglu, democracies win on the economic plane.

It is rather extraordinary to note that these two economists, having essentially the same instruments of analysis and the same training, come to such radically opposed conclusions. In the end, what should we make of the links between education, democracy and prosperity? Why do certain countries fall into the trap of poverty, corruption and dictatorship, while others follow the path of education, growth and democracy? Why does democracy survive in some countries (Great Britain in the 1930s) and collapse in others (Weimar Germany in the same period)?

The answer is rather simple, even if neither of the two protagonists really mentions it: democratic experience itself is the key that gives the measure of its robustness. The Weimar Republic was fragile because democracy was a new idea there. By contrast, Great Britain resisted because democratic ideas were already well anchored in public opinion and in institutions. Similarly, we may bet on India remaining democratic, although poor and under-educated. It is like appreciating opera: it takes a long apprenticeship to find pleasure in it. And if the industrial countries are all democratic, it is in large part because those of them that started out on another route, for instance Germany and Japan, were defeated militarily, much more than is due to the mechanical effects of prosperity on democratic aspirations.

In the end, one conclusion arises: Homo Politicus and Homo Economicus often encounter each other in human history, but their logics are not the same. Prosperity does not lead by its own qualities to democracy. This does not mean that economy and politics may ignore each other – on the contrary. Each constantly seeks its place relative to the other. But if China must change its political culture in the course of the twenty-first century, it is much more surely because the democratic idea will have crossed borders than because of the simple fact of higher material wealth. Globalization directly diffuses cultural and political models that go well beyond its economic effects alone.[30] If there exists one sterling virtue to growth, it is that it tends to open up borders, which allows ideas to cross over, too.

5

The Great Western Crisis

Sad Globalization

Globalization in the 1990s gave birth to hope for fresh world growth of which the emerging countries would be the locomotives. In the second half of the 1990s, all the forecasts were promising: unemployment dropped in the United States and in Europe, growth rates broke thresholds that recalled the postwar glory days. In France, three of the best five years for job creation over a century occurred in the years from 1997 to 2000. New markets, new technologies: everything seemed in place for a 'happy globalization'. How could it have derailed so quickly?

Much has been written on the origins of the financial crisis, from the greed of Wall Street to the impotence of politicians to do anything about it. But the central phenomenon relates to the fact that the United States had tried to resolve through debt the problems that it did not manage to solve economically. The dazzling rise in income disparities led the 1 per cent richest to capture two-thirds of the economic growth during the ten years that preceded the crisis.[1] Indebtedness had become the sole way for the middle and working classes to escape social relegation. Credit has taken the place of salaries.

How did this great country succeed in finding the necessary money? Thanks to a phenomenon that is no less strange. On the other side of the Pacific Ocean, in China, the rise in inequality has been just as spectacular. But the same causes do not produce the same effects there, and they have led the Chinese to constitute formidable precautionary savings. The accelerated ageing of the population, the absence of social protection and the absurd effects of the one-child policy have led the Chinese, especially the middle and upper classes, to hoard their new wealth in order to prepare for the future. The surplus savings of the poor country have thus permitted financing the deficit of the rich country. Here we might think of a film, *The Servant* by Joseph Losey, where the servant ends up dominating the master by making him addicted to his services.

Chinese 'mercantilism' has taught American liberalism a lesson. The mercantilist doctrine, elaborated in the seventeenth century, taught princes how to obtain commercial surpluses, find a way to bring gold into the national territory and possess the metal necessary to pay their armies. For mercantilists, the economy was itself a form of war, where the countries that sold more than they spent were the winners, and those who had a deficit were the losers. This doctrine was severely criticized by classic authors of the eighteenth century. The founders of economic liberalism, from Adam Smith to Ricardo via David Hume, would present international commerce as a 'positive sum' game: the one who buys *and* the one who sells *both* gain, as consumer and producer. Liberalism triumphed in England in the nineteenth century and in the United States somewhat later, in the course of the twentieth century.

Chinese mercantilism today resuscitates the old doctrines of the seventeenth century. Countries with a surplus assume power, which is quite simply that of the creditor over the debtor. In the strained geopolitics that began with the twenty-first century, the Chinese recalled an eternal lesson: it is better to be the ant than the grasshopper when the north wind blows. After the Second World War, the United States held credit notes for the rest of the world that put the country *de facto* in the position of being the 'world's banker'. Now the Chinese own United States' debts equivalent to 20,000 euros per American citizen! The dollar reigned after the war. Is the Yuan being prepared to play this strategic role?

The current crisis can be compared in many ways to that of 1929. According to Charles Kindleberger's interpretation, the Great Depression of the 1930s may be explained by the fact that the world did not have a 'lender of last resort' to contain the crisis.[2] America was not politically ready to play this role, and England no longer had the financial means. Today the question on everybody's lips is whether China is not in the situation in which America found itself between the two world wars. Already a financial power, it is not yet a political power at the global level. In this interpretation, we are living through an interregnum bearing all the attendant dangers, haunted by one question: will China continue to buy American debt much longer?

In another film, *Lawrence of Arabia* by David Lean, one of the British officers charged with watching over King Faisal sums up his demonstration of the causes of British superiority in a word repeated several times: 'discipline'. In a spectacular reversal of the situation, now it is the rich countries that demonstrate their *indiscipline*. The financial crisis that has struck the United States and Europe has handed the dunce's cap over to the advanced countries. At the summit of Cannes in November 2011, the emerging countries did not forego the pleasure of calling for more financial rigour there, asking the IMF that increased surveillance to be imposed on rich nations. The Western version of Homo Economicus has lost a little of his arrogance.

Europe in Distress

Chinese surpluses have made America more fragile. German surpluses have weakened the euro zone, ironically projecting Europe into the heart of the financial crisis. This is curious, because Europe was in no way the cause of the crisis, which owes much more to the imprudence of Wall Street. But quickly Europe took the route of the 1930s, getting bogged down in monetary and financial problems that it thought it had definitively solved. In fact, the financial and political pacification of the euro zone was revealed to be quite fragile. Jean Pisani-Ferry speaks of 'demons reawakened'. During the Greek crisis, mutual insults quickly accumulated in the scandal presses of Germany and Greece, which did not shrink from derogatory allusions to the other's past. The German ant accused the Greek grasshopper of not having foreseen the winter, and the latter accused the former of wanting to dominate Europe all over again.

Back in the 1930s, it was the French who occupied the position of creditor to the rest of Europe – and they proved to be stingy. When Austria entered into crisis in 1931, hit by the failure of the largest bank in the country (the Creditanstalt), France, which at the time had the largest stock of gold, delayed in answering calls for aid. England itself could not bear the shock provoked by the sudden uncertainty of financial markets. It had to give up the convertibility of the pound sterling into gold in September of the same year, unleashing the collapse of the monetary system of the time, the Gold Standard. Today, the euro has replaced gold as the monetary instrument, but in the end Europe finds itself faced with the same problems.

The European currency inherits the postwar debates about how to avoid a repetition of the crisis. During the Bretton Woods conference in 1944, the Allies had reflected (even before the end of the fighting) about a new international monetary system. Keynes, the famous English economist who led the British delegation, had stressed an essential point that we find at work today. The disequilibrium in the balance of payments is not 'symmetrical': the indebted country is much more vulnerable than the lending one. Countries in deficit should, sometimes even precipitately, reduce their style of living, without the countries in surplus being obliged to make a symmetrical effort to increase their own expenditures. Such asymmetry is a factor causing recession: if one country spends less without the other having to spend more, then the former's overall expenditure necessarily drops and unemployment increases.

Keynes had advocated the creation of a supranational currency (which he proposed calling the 'bancor') and the abandonment of gold (which he called a 'Barbarian relic'). Rather than spend the available yellow metal to guarantee the functioning of the international monetary system, he wanted a currency issued by a 'world bank' to respond to the liquidity needs of countries in deficit. His idea was openly fought by the Americans, for whom the world currency was *de facto* the dollar. But his idea did survive – in Europe. One of his disciples, Robert Triffin, a Belgian economist who would later teach at Yale University, became its standard bearer. And so convincing the Europeans that the creation of a supranational currency was the only way of avoiding the tyranny of the exchange market was an idea that caught on, from the Werner Plan in 1970 to the Delors Report in 1989, and would result in the euro.

By an astonishing paradox, today the euro has been transformed into a new golden prison, obliging European countries to undergo the same type of austerity as was conducted in the 1930s. One after another, Greece, Ireland, Portugal, then Spain, Italy and France have had to engage in severe budgetary purges to recover their international credit. The absurd spiral in which Europe once let itself become entrained was being repeated: to reduce deficits, but at the risk of breaking growth, then make up the shortfall in taxation power due to the recession by new measures of austerity. From 1930 to 1932, Chancellor Brüning, wanting to reassure the markets about Germany's creditworthiness, had conducted a policy of the same kind that would make the unemployment rate soar to stratospheric levels, greater than 25 per cent of the population. This figure was reached in 2012 by both Greece and Spain. In Germany, this policy would lead to a radicalization of political life, and then to Hitler's taking power in January 1933, less than four years after the crisis was triggered. In Greece, in the elections of May 2012, the Nazi Party ('Golden Dawn') re-entered Parliament.

In the United States, too, until the election of Roosevelt in 1933 the crisis would reach just as severe proportions and partly for the same reason: austerity policies aiming to re-establish confidence. Another important factor played in the American case that Milton Friedman would discuss in his book *A Monetary History of the United States*.[3] He thought that the gravity of the crisis of the 1930s related principally to the fact that the central Federal Reserve was then too young and too immature to have sufficient legitimacy to be able to eradicate the crisis. Created in 1913, the Fed was not up to its responsibilities. Without reacting, it let the American banking system implode in its face, and more than half the banks in the country went bankrupt during the crisis.

Here we may make a parallel with the European Central Bank, which abandoned European nations and condemned them to market exposure, no doubt for the same reason as the Fed in its day: a young institution worried about its credibility did not dare act as it should have. While it possessed the means to break the speculation against various nations, the European Central Bank quickly let it be known that it would not play the role of 'lender of last resort'. The 'money printer' was not activated; here German traumatic fear of the hyperinflation of the 1920s acted as a formidable blocking factor, even when the inflationary risks were non-existent.

Treaties formally forbid the ECB from lending directly to states. But it may intervene on the secondary market. The ECB thus set up a programme to buy back public debt during the months of May 2010 and August 2011. After these interventions, the president of the Bundesbank, Axel Weber, resigned, along with his chief economist, Jurgen Stark – which put an end to the exercise. When Mario Draghi was appointed to the ECB, he conducted a policy of massive credit to the banks, in the hope that they would lend to the nation-states. (It would have sufficed if he had been able to lend directly to them to stifle the crisis.) Without intervention, the pressure exerted by the markets on fragile member countries (Greece, Ireland, Portugal), then on the majority of member countries (Italy, Spain, France notably, but also Belgium and Austria) gradually became oppressive. Austerity was imposed on fragile countries, creating a remedy that was worse than the malady. Thus in an extraordinary turnaround of the situation, the euro thus acted as the gold standard once had, locking down economic policy, even though it had originally been conceived to avoid the perverse effects of currency competition.

Technicians who were determined not to make 'policy' (an attitude in the spirit if not the letter of treaties) were managing the European currency – which was what doomed Europe. Beyond the monetary episodes, which have the annoying tendency of repeating themselves, it is really the whole idea of European construction that has been shaken.

The pioneers of its edification, from the Community of Coal and Steel created in 1951 until the creation of the euro in 1999, have always thought that economic integration would lead to political integration. This has not occurred. The error in reasoning is the same one committed by those who think about China: notably, that economic prosperity leads to democracy. If one had wanted to develop European citizenship, one would have started off differently: favouring much more the learning of European languages, raising by a factor of ten the number of educational and university exchanges, and in this way fostering mixed marriages, would have made people's mobility infinitely more simple from the standpoint of employment and social security.

Buying German cars or Italian suits in no way fosters a feeling of belonging to a shared community. In fact, when the crisis was raging, it actually produced the opposite sentiment. Economic rivalry sharpens national rivalries, and reopens old wounds that were thought to have healed. Homo Economicus can quickly become bitter, if not vindictive.

De-Industrialization

As a result of the crisis, more than half of Americans and of Europeans now think that globalization is responsible for it, that globalization makes more jobs to be lost rather than gained, that it is a factor accounting for rising inequalities. Economists are often disoriented in the face of these critiques. The speed with which industrial employment has been destroyed is certainly impressive. Between 1980 and 2010, the share of industry (in terms of number of hours worked) went from 23 per cent to 15 per cent in Europe and from 19 per cent to 10 per cent in the United States. In France, 5.3 million people worked in industry in 1980, but they were no more than 3.4 million in 2010. However, econometric study has a great deal of difficulty in discerning a significant impact of commercial openness on the unemployment rate.

According to a recent study that summarizes a majority of this econometric work, the losses directly linked to world trade represent in France 13 per cent of some 71,000 industrial jobs lost on average each year between 1980 and 2007, meaning that globalization accounts for about 10,000 jobs lost each year.[4] Since the 2000s, the number of jobs destroyed has increased, rising to almost 18,000 per year. These are significant figures. But even when confined to the industrial sector alone (which is the most exposed to international competition), the effects of commerce remain largely behind other factors in destroying jobs, which account for 85 per cent of the total.

The central paradox of industrial employment, which repeats the evolution of agricultural employment in the course of the early twentieth century, is that its disappearance relates to its actual success. When a sector experiences overly rapid productivity gains, it tends to disappear! Productivity measures the number of products made (in an hour, for example) by each worker. When it increases in one sector more rapidly than in the rest of the economy, then the offer of goods (here industrial) becomes too abundant in relation to other social needs. Employment must migrate from the highly productive sector towards one that is less so. This explains the rural exodus yesterday, and the industrial exodus today. The farming population went from 80 per cent to one per cent, yet the physical production by no means diminished! Such is the fate today of industry, whose share constantly declines due to the effect of productivity gains that ever more reduce the demand for labour.

The rise in industrial productivity, which is in itself a factor of progress (more goods are produced in less time) thus becomes the principal cause of the dropping employment in this sector. Despite the fall in its personnel, industry still accounts for a significant share of growth (0.8 per cent per year in Europe, 0.7 per cent in the United States over the last thirty years).[5] In theory, nothing opposes the shift of labour from one sector to another. Yesterday the jobs lost by agriculture were gained by industry. By the same reasoning, today tertiary jobs might replace industrial jobs. But this transition is a formidable factor of fragility, which requires an active economic policy of support for the retraining of the unemployed and for the overall demand. The crisis becomes systemic when economic policy loses its own operating levers. Then the transition becomes brutal; the triumph of growth is transformed into a tragedy.

However, certain countries seem to manage better than others to preserve industrial employment. Among the rich countries this is the case with Germany and Japan that have managed, thanks to the dynamism of their exports, to preserve an industrial force. These two countries illustrate the industrial paradox in another way. Job protection in this sector is impossible within the framework of an economy that is closed to international exchanges. Withdrawn into its own market alone, an economy would quickly be deprived of outlets, and the law of increasing productivity would lead only to the lowering of employment. Industry might survive, but only if it is able to export its surplus. Here we touch on one of the sources of 'industrial mercantilism': the country most aggressive about exporting may impose on the others a de-industrialization that it can avoid itself. Already, in the nineteenth century, England entirely gambled its industrialization on a growth strategy for its exports, augmenting in a concomitant way its agricultural imports. The other countries denounced the unequal exchange that this division of roles established.

According to Ricardo's reasoning, it suffices for workers to migrate from the sector in decline to the one that is developing in order for everybody to gain, whether importer or exporter of industrial goods.[6] The reality is obviously much less rosy. The hiring capacity of exporting sectors is not unlimited. In a recent reformulation of theories of international trade, Melitz, Eaton and Kortum (who are today the leaders of the field) explicitly take this point into account. Exchanges principally take place through the phenomenon of elimination of the weakest and expansion of the strongest.[7] Trade, by destroying the least efficient firms, contributes to increasing the productivity of the whole. The annoying consequence, in the framework of these new theories, is that the survivors' capacity of driving forward the whole economy is limited. The best firms cannot hire all the losers, as was in principle the case in Ricardo's day. Globalization leaves its traces of debris. Hence, in this new interpretation, international trade functions according to a neo-Darwinian logic, where the most precarious competitors disappear and the best prosper, without market forces being sufficient to offer the former a guaranteed re-insertion into the economy. Now the question becomes whether accompanying mechanisms are possible that would allow the winners to rescue the losers. And when the answer is negative, then globalization quickly becomes unacceptable to people.

Planetary Isolation

In an article full of irony, a French economist specializing in raw materials posed the question: 'What is there in common between Elizabeth Taylor's jewels, a bottle of vintage wine, and a football player?' The answer is that all three beat price records during the year 2011.[8] The price of the best Bordeaux was beaten in Hong Kong; the jewels at Christie's auction house in London; and huge football players owe their salaries to the fascination of Russian oligarchs and to the petrodollars of Qatar. These three items (jewels, wine, sport) are the most caricatured facets of globalization.

Much more serious is the breathtaking rise in the prices of raw materials, such as the ten-fold increase in the price of a barrel of oil in ten years, which are as spectacular as these hikes in conspicuous consumption. 'Elevated prices', writes Philippe Chalmin, 'reflect the reality of a situation in which the planet lives on credit, this time in terms of resources.'

The enrichment of emerging countries poses problems for the Western world that go well beyond destroyed jobs: it considerably reinforces the demand for rare resources. The benefits of globalization seem to have been positive overall in terms of purchasing power until 2005–6. Consumers were able to have access to manufactured goods that were less expensive, like flat screens and smartphones . . . But with the sharp rise in the cost of raw materials (like petroleum), the benefit of the lower prices of imported industrial products was lost. One of the side-effects of this growing cost of raw materials has been to oblige the advanced countries to export more to pay for their imports. Industry, which represents 80 per cent of world trade, here regained its key role: it allowed paying for non-renewable resources.

Raw materials are only part of the problem, however. Climatic disturbances and the dangers linked to new epidemics create much more worrying planetary risks. Since the start of the 1970s, the number of natural and human catastrophes has tripled. According to the insurance company Swissre,[9] two-thirds of the twenty-five most costly catastrophes (for the insurance companies) of the last forty years have occurred since 2001 under the effects of climatic disturbances.

The threat of pandemics also figures among the new planetary risks. According to the OECD, a pandemic of influenza-A is one of the most important threats for the future of humanity: 'very contagious diseases, difficult or impossible to cure, which spread in a world that is more and more interconnected.' These risks are not new, of course. They evoke the great plague of the fourteenth century, in the course of which 30 to 50 per cent of the European population died, or the Spanish flu of 1918–19 that caused from 40 to 50 million deaths. But they assume a new urgency with globalization. In 2002, the SARS virus that had infected one person in a Hong Kong hotel immediately spread. Modern air transport now permits an infectious disease to travel in a few days from one corner of the globe to another. The H1N1 virus, which could have killed two to seven million people, shows the speed of diffusion thanks to globalization. The experts seem to agree about the fact that the principal epidemiological risk will come in a new form of influenza-A, for which there will be little or no possible immunity, circulating very fast and easily from person to person.[10]

In these extreme situations, the measures to be taken to fight against epidemics might go so far as to offer anti-viral medicines to 80 per cent of the threatened population. Other measures include closing borders and restricting people's mobility, demanding that they remain at home. These measures are very complex, politically, to put into effect. Back in 1976, the United States experienced a first bird flu. Worried about the outbreak of a new Spanish flu, the government launched a programme of national vaccination. Shortly after the programme got underway, it appeared that the 'bird flu' in fact presented no danger. Meanwhile 40 million Americans had already been vaccinated, with some of them suffering serious side-effects, which unleashed protests and lawsuits.

While they are worrying in themselves, epidemiological risks are also a perfect metaphor for the threats that hover over the world, whether financial crises or Internet viruses. Of course, financial crises are not new. But the statistics assembled by economists show that, like natural catastrophes, they have not stopped increasing.[11] The sub-prime crisis showed the new permeability of the international financial sphere to the spread of toxic products. Adulterated products like those derived from bad assets like dubious mortgages move around at the speed of lightning from one country to another. There comes a critical moment when doubt spreads: 'what if my neighbour carries the virus?' In the case of sub-primes, the inter-banking market suddenly dried up during the summer of 2007 due to this concern. Financial globalization is a powerful factor in the systemic fragility. When everything is going well, it seems that it always will go well; euphoria gains ground. When everything is going badly, everything can collapse in a second.[12]

These kinds of crises have the same source: networks whose interconnectivity produces extreme pathologies in response to certain perturbations. It is characteristic of these shocks to ricochet in a universe where non-linearity is the rule. Suddenly, a system may malfunction, like an electricity grid that plunges a city into darkness due to an incident that was initially minor. Complex systems obey statistical laws that make 'rare events' rather 'frequent'. And thus it goes with financial, epidemiological and Internet crises, which are new threats hanging over an interconnected world – and in the face of which the community of nations seems quite disarmed.

Therefore we are breaking through a new frontier of complexity. Should we fear that this is one complexity threshold too many? Optimists argue that the evolution of life has always been in this direction. Life yesterday always seems more peaceful because in fact it was simpler; each generation has the same experience. But the idea that complexity might be good in itself because it is 'natural' is totally false. The proposition that humankind has 'always' resisted the rise in the risks it has triggered is a bad argument. Many civilizations have indeed disappeared in the past (the Mayas, Sumer, Easter Island) because they have not been able to respond to the ecological challenges they themselves caused. We cannot manage to believe that we might be in the same situation and so we put our faith in science and nation-states to prevent the worst. But science is uncertain and nations are led by governments more bent on reducing people's discontent in the here-and-now than on anticipating future crises.

6

Darwin's Nightmare

Homo Numericus

Globalization is definitely a hybrid process. It manufactures crises reminiscent of the 1930s, awakens nationalist passions and reanimates a mercantilism that interprets commerce as a war among nations. But it is also the theatre of a new planetary society, totally interconnected, which causes new pathologies to arise that evoke the great epidemics of the Middle Ages.

In the new cybernetic world, the Internet takes the role played yesterday by electricity, organizing in radically new ways spaces of both production and social experience. Yesterday, television, the daughter of electricity, was installed in households and deftly overturned lifestyles. Putnam accused it of having broken down the 'social capital' of Americans, provoking a spurt of individualism that then played a role in the acceptance of inequalities.[1] Today, the social networks in turn redesign public space. How can we interpret them; can we hope that they are preparing a resurrection of civic spirit?

For Putnam himself the answer is negative. 'Virtual communities' are for him a contradiction in terms. He thinks the Internet is still in a state of nature close to that described by Hobbes. In fact there are two contradictory tendencies at work in the Internet today. One is related to television, and the other to the telephone; they pull in opposite directions. The film *Social Network* shows what led Mark Zuckerberg to invent Facebook. Organizing an on-line beauty competition for Harvard students, he discovered that its success related to the fact that the participants voted for girls they had already met. So he concluded that Facebook connects people who know each other! The same 'discovery' had been made with the telephone. Of course it allowed people to call the four corners of the globe, but most communication took place among people in the same town. In the language of economists, the telephone is actually a good that is 'complementary' to proximity, not a 'substitute' for it.[2] As today with the Internet, the geography of telephonic links is very close to geography itself.[3] Graham Bell, who invented the telephone in 1876, was himself totally blind to the transformations that his invention was going to enable. He imagined that it was playing a role much closer to that played by the radio somewhat later. For a whole generation, according to valuable data supplied by Antonio Casilli, there was a divorce between the way in which the role of the telephone was theorized and the uses made of it in practice.[4] Notably, it was thought that the telephone would serve only businesses and be used scarcely at all for private conversations!

Facebook introduced an innovation that at the time was underestimated: it enlarged bilateral discussions to multilateral discussions. The change seemed minor, but it overturned the nature of the medium. The digital world pushed back what was specific to the modern world: the right to intimacy, to privacy.[5] In agricultural societies, where the conditions of existence were related to perpetual overpopulation, intimacy was beyond reach. Not until the modern world did there appear a 'security distance' (Hannah Arendt) between each person and everyone else. This distance is today being reduced. The right to forget who you were also disappears. Whoever at age twenty attends a wild party will have to assume the consequences his or her whole life long . . .

In certain aspects, Homo Numericus restores ancient conceptions of the personality. As Jean-Pierre Vernant stressed, the Greek man experienced everything in 'exteriority' – under and for the gaze of others, being a 'he' before being an 'I'. The digital world creates a new social life in which users subject themselves to the constant regard of others, in effect returning to a pre-modern definition of individuality. How should we understand this voluntary servitude? According to Antonio Casilli,[6] we should speak instead of 'participatory surveillance', distinct from that exercised from above by a Big Brother. A user fabricates an on-line space that allows him to manage the flows of information that are useful to him. In the end, though, the relation of the self with others is totally modified. A new social addiction is created.

But the Internet also creates another world, a subterranean one, with rules totally distinct from those that are imposed on a network like Facebook. It allows acting behind a mask, under a pseudonym (often several of them), which radically modifies the rules of the social game. On the Internet, 'nobody knows that you are a dog', in the famous *New Yorker* cartoon. Philip Rosedale has created the concept of 'second life' to characterize this new universe where you can act via an interposed avatar.[7] A study of the Japanese case as analysed by Antonio Casilli demonstrates the new type of society that arises when individuals act under the veil of anonymity. The '2 Channel' (*nichanneru*) site, where all the actors are disguised by pseudonyms, has become one of the most populated in the world, with 2.5 million subscribers.

It reveals a face of Japanese society that is exactly the inverse of what is shown by the light of day, where the Japanese are habitually modest, respectful of hierarchies, etc. The site is one of the least presentable in the world, featuring illegal pornography, libels against private and public persons, crude vulgarity in language. Millions of users without faces can escape the risk of 'losing face'.

Cybersex is an example among others of the pathologies born in the anonymous world of the Internet. A study in the same spirit called 'The Internet and Life Satisfaction'[8] shows that the time spent on the Internet often correlates with solitude and the *least* satisfaction. More than 13,000 people chosen randomly answered a questionnaire (in 2004 and 2005). One hour spent on the Internet correlated with five times more solitude than one hour spent with friends. Even the frequent use of e-mail is an indicator of solitude. The study obviously does not show that the Internet *causes* solitude. It is probably the opposite: solitude is a cause of the frequent use of the Internet. But it seems that we cannot get rid of either one.

Darwin and the Economists

The emerging digital society thus produces a new figure of the individual: a being that seems deprived of a clear awareness of itself, simultaneously in exteriority, under the constant gaze of others, and in inferiority performing under multiple masks the unsatisfied portion of his or her fantasies. Inspired no doubt by the world of Facebook, Roland Benabou and Jean Tirole[9] (the two economists who studied the perverse effects of rewards to children) put back to work the classic model of Homo Economicus, by including among his calculations (beyond money) a concern to have a good image presented to others. As in the writings of the eighteenth-century philosopher La Rochefoucauld, they find that disinterestedness becomes 'interested': it aims to attract the recognition of others.

In the model proposed, the concern to gain the respect of others is organized like a zero-sum game: those who are admired win the social war against those who are not. The former overreact to social codes, the latter abandon them. This social game tends to create (to adopt Robert Castel's analysis) two pathologies: the 'individual by default', who loses footing in the social game, and the 'individual by excess', who imputes to himself alone the causes of his success, disdaining other people.

In this respect this model is perfectly part of the current climate, representative of a competition whose stakes are not only winning (more or less) but also asserting oneself socially. It incarnates a new way of conceiving life in society, already encountered in our analysis of the industrial world, where only the most skilful can survive. But by turning to Darwinian metaphors like the 'struggle for life', society is actually fabricating a new ideology, and there is nothing 'natural' about it.

Darwin himself dedicated his first book to an economist, Thomas Malthus, the proponent of population theory. Malthus enunciated a profoundly sad theory of human societies. According to him, the natural law of demography is an ineluctable obstacle to any improvement in prosperity. As soon as people lift themselves above the subsistence level, then mortality recedes, the birth-rate increases, and eventually demographic pressure sets in. The number of humans increases, to the point that the available (food) resources are lacking. If a man cannot feed his family, writes Malthus, 'they must starve or be left to the support of casual bounty'. For Malthus, it was an illusion to want to reduce the suffering of the poor. They would merely have more children, and then demographic pressure would take away with one hand that which the other nourishing hand had given them.

Darwin in the introduction to *The Origin of Species* takes up this intuition.[10] 'More individuals [of each species] are born than can possibly survive [. . .] Only those variations which are in some way profitable will be preserved or naturally selected [. . .] In the survival of favoured individuals and races, during the constantly recurrent Struggle for Life, we see a powerful and ever-acting force of Selection.' Thus a law of nature takes shape: a struggle for existence in the course of which the weakest and less organized must succumb to extinction.

The temptation to use these theories for social ends quickly became fashionable in the nineteenth century, before falling into disrepute in the twentieth. Jean-Claude Ameisen recalls that in the nineteenth century, Darwinism was not long in breaking through the boundaries of natural biology to tip over into racism.[11] Francis Galton, the founder of eugenics, proposed a theory of the selection of species applied to humans, which he soberly explained: 'What Nature does blindly, slowly and brutally, man can do on purpose rapidly and gently.'[12] No country has been spared by these ideas. In France, Alexis Carrell (Nobel Prize-winner in Medicine in 1912) proposed replacing democracy by 'biocracy'. . . In the United States a law was passed in 1924 that imposed a drastic reduction in the entry of immigrants from southern and Eastern Europe in order to protect the American nation from the propagation of their 'hereditary defects'. The American Eugenics Society was created in 1926. As Ameisen stresses, most of the great scientists who supported the theory of evolution would also support social Darwinism, or else keep quiet. It was not until the start of the 1940s, with the gradual discovery of what Nazism meant in this regard, that these associations dissolved themselves. Eugenics would be finally discredited, but by wars more than by the moral conscience of peoples and their savants . . .

Darwin distrusted what he perceived as bad uses of his theories. If he borrowed from Malthus the notion of 'struggle for existence', he also added that it should be extended only in a metaphorical direction. In *The Genealogy of Man*, he insisted on the existence of phenomena of cooperation among individuals of the same species, including humankind, which he called sociability, cooperation and 'sympathy'. In his eyes, the essential 'novelty' of humankind was not the struggle for survival, or even intelligence, but the existence of a capacity for attention to the other. Altruism or sympathy, this 'noblest part of our nature' that natural selection has caused to emerge, should lead us to refuse the blind action of natural selection.

Darwin had also read *The Theory of Moral Sentiments*, written by another economist, Adam Smith, who opens the book with 'On Sympathy: 'How selfish soever man may be supposed, there are evidently some principles in his nature, which interest him in the fortunes of others and render their happiness necessary to him, though he derives nothing from it except the pleasure of seeing it.' Darwin seems to have taken the opposite road to Smith, who would be the founder of modern economic science. Smith in that first book proposed a vision of man oriented towards the quest for the sympathy of others. But in his more famous second book, *The Wealth of Nations*, he expounded a point of view that was exactly the opposite, explaining that it was better to organize society by betting on selfishness rather than on generosity.

Reading these two writers together and following their hesitations, one conclusion stands out. In the subtle equilibrium between competition and cooperation, nothing permits us to say that the former is more 'natural' than the latter. Experiments like the Trust Game, analysed in an earlier chapter, recall the force of the 'natural' propensity of humans to reciprocity.

The Selfish Gene

Despite the warnings of Darwin himself, many researchers, consumed with a perfectly respectable scientific project, have wanted to flush out what is 'properly human' by looking at the animal kingdom. According to some of them, there is at most a difference of degree between the so-called traits specific to humans and their proto-manifestations among animals.[13] Humans are made up of 98 per cent of the same genes as the chimpanzee or the bonobo,[14] our cousins with whom we share a common ancestor back seven to ten million years ago. What does that teach us about humankind, and what do we know about our genes?

The principal statistical indications about their role come from the comparison between true and false twins. The Minnesota Twins Registry offers a multitude of data. For example, we learn that in the case of identical twins, if one suffers from schizophrenia, the other has a 47 per cent chance of suffering from it also. But if they are only fraternal twins, the probability falls to 17 per cent. If one of them is an alcoholic, the identical twin has a probability of 41 per cent, the fraternal one of 22 per cent. In short, a major pathological trait has one chance in two of being found in an identical twin, and one chance in five of being found in a fraternal twin. Distinguishing between cases where the two twins were raised together or separately was used to test the results. This study brutally reintroduced the question of heredity, the heaviest of the chains from which modern people thought they were liberated . . .

In a book that had worldwide success, *The Selfish Gene* (which sold more than a million copies), Richard Dawkins presents genes as the veritable masters of life, since humans (like other species) are guided by the imperious desire to reproduce themselves. The male spider lets himself be devoured during copulation by the female spider in order to feed the latter and give every chance to its progeny. The concern of parents for children is thus only an avatar of programming designed to make our genes grow, like a company that makes its capital bear fruit.

Modern man seems to depend on progress in genetics to understand his intimate nature. We anxiously await the result of comparisons once considered as exotic, like that which separates us from the Neanderthal, the closest 'cousin' to the human species, with whom we cohabited until 30,000 years ago. We share with him 99.8 per cent of our genes, but it appears that we are separated by some fundamental differences, too. Neanderthal man stood upright, was fully biped, mastered tools just like us, and no doubt had metaphysical preoccupations, since he was also given to funerary rites. But Neanderthal man left no work of art. Though contemporary with our ancestors of Lascaux, it seems he did not possess the same kind of imagination as the cave painters. It has been noted that the big monkeys do not look each other in the eyes. It is possible that this was also the case with Neanderthal. Is looking each other in the eye specific to humans, as the philosopher Emmanuel Levinas thought?

In 2006, the primatologist Frans de Waal[15] took up this theme. He argued that empathy – which consists of feeling inside oneself the suffering of another – is not the point of arrival but the point of departure of human history. It is not culture that makes us social, but our predisposition to seek others that makes social life possible. Giacomo Rizzolatti, who discovered the biological supports underlying empathy, says that they reveal 'how deeply anchored in us is the link that attaches us to others'.[16] Is this (at last) what is specific to humankind? It does not seem so. The same markers have been found in the Rhesus monkey.[17] At least here we see that the propensity for cooperation, reciprocity and empathy form an essential dimension of 'human nature' – if we have to use that word.

But even the fanatics of 'selfish gene' theories do not go so far as to assert that genes predetermine our identity. Genes do influence our ways of responding to pressures from an environment.[18] To think that we may untangle the part owed to the environment from the part owed to genetic predispositions is a formidable intellectual challenge, but it seems quite vain. We are close to both chimpanzees and bonobos by our genes. Chimpanzees are patriarchal societies that are structured around dominant males. Bonobos are matriarchal societies with dominant females and exuberant sexual activity. Which do we resemble? This is an absurd question, obviously, but many are those who would like to give an answer!

Francis Wolff, in a wide-ranging study subtitled 'From Aristotle to the Neurosciences', deals brilliantly with all these questions.[19] In a certain way, he explains, we have returned to the debate about origins that was already present in Aristotle, who held that man was a 'rational animal', meaning two things at once. He is an animal among others, a biped with arms and hands where others have wings or fins. But he is also capable of reason, for he possesses language. In this respect he is close to the gods, except for one point: he is mortal. But 'unlike animals that are ignorant of the question, and gods who don't care about it, man has perceptions of good and evil, the just and the unjust, and other notions of this type'. Thus man has the privilege over other animals of being able to live 'reasonably', by mastering his emotions, in harmony with other humans. This leads Aristotle to conclude that man is 'by nature' a political animal, which allows us to include in this compact formula the two terms encountered in Charles Darwin and Adam Smith.

Genetic theories certainly do open fascinating scientific horizons. But their philosophic scope must be relativized. According to Wolff, to say 'that "man is an animal like the others" is a self-contradictory phrase – if it is true, the fact that man says it proves that he is *not* an animal like the others! Monkeys may speak, perhaps, but they do not have theories about monkeys! While man-as-object loses his singularity, man-as-subject of said knowledge triumphs!' A human learns, understands, evolves, compares himself to others. For these reasons, his history is always open, for better or worse, to an undefined future. Wolff concludes, 'A human is neither good nor bad. He is capable of devotion and of barbarism. But he is the only animal that asks the question.' In the end, the singularity of humans is evident, even up to and including when they think they are demonstrating there is no such thing![20]

The Genetic Body

The scientific revolution of Galileo and Newton in the seventeenth century had already overthrown traditional conceptions of the place of humans in nature and the universe. But it had also – perhaps especially – prepared the industrial revolution of the eighteenth century, opening the way to modern capitalism. Just like today: if the genetic revolution overthrows philosophical conceptions about humankind, it also prepares a new kind of industrial revolution. Here it is not machines, but the bodies of human beings made of flesh and blood that are its instruments.

Ray Kurzweil in a book titled *The Singularity is Near: When Humans Transcend Biology* (2005) heralded for 2060 nothing less than an abrupt transition in the human species. He thinks a trans-human world is about to come. Each human will have new organs to sustain his intelligence, lengthen his lifespan and perhaps attain immortality . . . Kurzweil (whose name makes one think of a film by Stanley Kubrick) made a rather astonishing splash. Interviewed by Roger-Pol Droit and Monique Atlan for their study

L'Humain, this prophet of neo-futurism was prepared to wager on a progressive improvement in mechanisms that will enable the body to be 'regenerated' and to postpone ageing.

The great worry of Ray Kurzweil is that he might die a few years too early, before the great bifurcation of the humanity occurs, when science will make immortality possible. Other scholars confirm his prognosis. 'Just as there are blood stem cells that will always produce blood cells, or muscle stem cells, we discover that there are neural stem cells. There is a potential for regenerating the brain, conserving at least a fraction of our population of neurons, which are always a fraction of the juvenile, even embryonic neurons.'

Beyond the modifications made *in vivo* to the human being, should we fear that, with the progress of *in vitro* fertilization, the selection of the 'best' baby might become possible? The debate on stem cells illustrates the complexity of these coming choices. Stem cells are 'pluripotent' cells: they have the power to be transformed into any type of cell in the organism. Adversaries of these techniques have pointed out that one has to destroy an embryo (hence a potential human being) to create stem cells. This debate has now been decided in favour of genetic research. But it is less the lost embryo that is disturbing than the use that could be made of it. If stem cells may allow us to defeat the maladies of old age such as Parkinson's and Alzheimer's, very well . . . But then could we long resist cloning, or the manufacturing of artificial DNA sequences for the purpose of adding to cells some functions not found in nature? Already Texan millionaires dream of making clones, consumed by the crazy project of progeny in their own image (perfect, of course!), and perhaps also by the dream of possessing an organ bank that would allow them to reach the trans-human future promised by Kurzweil.

The sequencing of the human genome was the grand affair of the final years of the last century. The quantity of information borne by DNA chains is not overwhelming: three billion bytes, or the digital coding of a two-hour film. Each person will soon be able to procure a DVD with the total sequence of his or her genome. Will we one day have to submit a DVD on which one's genome sequence is written in order to find a job or obtain insurance? The anonymous CV might soon seem like the Maginot Line in the face of the coming torrent.

Many are those who today wager that the century will witness a convergence between human intelligence and non-biologic intelligence. The US Department of Defense has invested millions of dollars in studying the connection between computers and the human brain. Science fiction nourishes many fantasies on the relation of people with machines. In Stanley Kubrick's film, *2001: A Space Odyssey* (1968), the robot HAL tries to beat humans on the terrain of intelligence, just like Big Blue, the IBM computer, beat the world chess champion, Gary Kasparov. The film *Blade Runner* (1982), based on a novel by Philip K. Dick, goes even further: the detective charged with detecting genetic robots falls in love with one of the creatures he is supposed to be hunting down. The founder of computing, Alan Turing, foresaw that by 2000 machines would be capable of fooling 30 per cent of humans on the following test: conversing via computer with someone, in how many cases would the human understand that he was actually talking with a robot? Yet up to now no machine has managed to pass this test.

This figure of the robot who acts in the place of humans should not be confused with another scenario that is fundamentally distinct: a human whose functions are enhanced by medications or grafts. The film *Limitless* (2011) tells the story of an ordinary man who discovers (thanks to very powerful pills) that he can use his concentration and his memory much more effectively. Here it is the human who remains in command, using machines or medications to multiply his own power. In the previous case the machine was a substitute, but here it becomes complementary to the human. In the match between Gary Kasparov and Big Blue, some argued that the IBM computer must have had human help. What is certain is that the pairing of Big Blue plus Kasparov is much more formidable than one of them on its own!

For economists, these evolutions may be interpreted as the promise of a new model of growth, which Robert Boyer calls 'anthropogenic'. Economic history may shed light on its possible nature. Humans long worked the land, then they worked on matter and today they are becoming their own object. All the predictions made at the start of the nineteenth century heralded that machines were going to impoverish workers since they were going to replace them. But later history proved – on the contrary – that they enabled a *rise* in workers' salaries. The machine functions like Archimedes' lever: it multiplies a human's productive force, which allows the person who uses it to earn more. So if economic history must be used to illuminate the future, it seems that it is wiser to bet on instruments that will make humans more efficient, whatever the (potentially terrible) definition of those instruments, rather than bet that robots will come along to compete with us. Thus economic theory validates the intuitions of *Limitless* rather than those of *Blade Runner* (running counter to their respective artistic merits): the future holds a high-performance human with increased potentialities.

The Church in its time had to withdraw behind lines of defence when the science of Galileo and Newton exploded its conception of the world. Today, it is the turn of humanists to set their line of defence far behind the rupture that is looming. Aldo Schiavone proposed this defence: that all the modifications brought to the body or the brain be non-transmissible to following generations, so that humans would be left unchanged.[21] This deliberately provocative idea reveals the fragility of our humanist certitudes in the face of the cybernetic chasm.

7

The Postmodern Condition

The Late-Modern World

The digital society and the genetic revolution are at the centre of the ruptures that are capable of carrying human societies far from their traditional bases. This new world, full of both promises and uncertainties, is still largely disconnected from the world experienced by the majority of people, who remain absorbed by questions of purchasing power, jobs, housing . . . A hiatus has been created between the potentialities of the technological world and its concrete realizations, which remain feeble. This gap between the world to come and the present world is reinforced by an additional frustration: even the old hopes borne by the modern world are also languishing.

A premonitory book by Jean-François Lyotard, *La Condition postmoderne* (*The Postmodern Condition*, 1984),[1] explained magnificently the tenor of this confusion. According to Lyotard, modernity might be interpreted as the moment in history when the cause of freedom triumphs in all domains: political, cultural and economic. Postmodernity describes the world *after* this conquest has taken place, when the struggles for freedom give way to nostalgia for the fights waged in order to obtain it. Lyotard notes that our era marks the exhaustion of the great myths carried by the modern world, like the French Revolution and German idealism, decolonization and sexual emancipation, in which man became the 'heroic agent of his own liberation'. The post-modern world comes along to put an end to history as it is recounted in textbooks – the conquest of a better world, liberated from political or economic tyrannies.

In the political domain, according to this interpretation, emancipation is already achieved now that the model of representative democracy is dominant. Political passions have been spent. This will be the theme (but ten years later) of the theory of Francis Fukuyama concerning the 'end of history'. In the economic domain, freedom from the 'con-straints of necessity' (to speak like Hannah Arendt) is like-wise achieved. Now fully fed and housed, modern humans have only to amuse themselves. Therefore social classes have lost their pertinence. But new 'oppositional' poles of identity do arise. According to Lyotard, they no longer relate to classes, but rather to gender, race, ecology and sexual orien-tation . . .. Nature makes a return in the same nostalgic register, to be integrated into a new culture. 'Truth is a moment of falsehood', said Guy Debord in what he called *La Société du spectacle* (1967).[2] The athlete on steroids, the woman with cosmetic surgery, the cloning of Texan million-aires – today these are the triumphant figures.

The old conflicts between left and right are also affected. Rafaële Simone[3] recounts this twist with humour, in a perfectly postmodern way. He explains that modernity deliv-ered an immense hope, of which the Left was the standard bearer since it defines itself as the progressive camp. The Right incarnates reaction, the defence of pre-modern values like authority and religion. Yesterday the Right was 'out' and the Left 'in'. But in a way unanticipated by its former

conservative values, the Right finds itself more at ease than
the Left with the world of today. Whether regarding 'advertising, easy credit, the desire for fun, an escape, the hope to
remain young (including on the sexual plane) – in all these
domains the Right is "trendy" and the Left is gloomy and
out'. For Simone, in an entertainment society where inhibi-
tions are lowered, to be on the Left appears like a 'renuncia-
tion'. He thinks that basically the Right has come back to
simple ideas: 'Nature is good: fun, enjoyment, wellness,
resorts.' Entertainment has become a political right.

These statements bear the mark of the era in which they
were written, when Berlusconi was in power in Italy, and
now they already seem out of date during our era of crisis
and austerity . . . Lyotard's theory is itself much more profound than the announcement of a society of entertainment.
But under Simone's veil of irony appear some misunderstandings raised by *The Postmodern Condition*. The triumph
of freedom that the book seemed to announce is more
ambiguous than it appears. By becoming a norm of modernity, freedom becomes an imperative injunction: 'you *must*
be autonomous!' – an obligation as much as a consolation.

But the most delicate issue is whether we have really
managed to liberate ourselves from the constraints of necessity, meaning from material needs. For the paradox of the
current age relates to the almost inverse situation. The death
of the revolutionary 'grand narratives', their epilogue in the
fall of the Berlin Wall, the 'end of ideologies', as it is also
called – results not in a postmaterialist society, but on the
contrary in a society that is actually becoming more
materialist.

A Postmaterialist Society?

An idea has long circulated that the enrichment of societies
always triggers an 'elevation' in how needs are structured.

In the 1940s, the psychologist Alfred Maslow offered a theory that human needs form a pyramid with several levels. When a person lives at the limits of physiological existence, nourishment is the primordial need he tries to satisfy – and of course it eclipses all others. The second fundamental good is physical security. Not to be killed at the street corner is one of the very first needs to be satisfied, although a famished creature will take the risk of getting killed in order to eat. When these two needs are guaranteed, according to Maslow, higher needs will appear. They include three levels that run from the need for a family life and friends, up to the concern for the recognition of others, and finally peaking at full 'self-realization', fulsome knowledge of oneself and the world . . . In the same vein, Virginia Henderson has proposed fourteen levels (!), running from the same fundamental needs like eating and surviving, to higher needs that also include entertainment.

These theories, which guided advertising and marketing in the 1950s, are supposed to illuminate ascending human aspirations. In fact, we do see in the statistics an evolution in household expenditure: the share devoted to food is reduced, while that devoted to leisure increases. In the course of the last fifty years in France food has gone from 38 per cent in 1960 to 25 per cent of disposable income, where it stands today, while the share devoted to leisure, culture and communication rose from 10 per cent to 16 per cent. And of course the higher a person rises in the income scale, the more this evolution becomes manifest.

For Richard Easterlin (the author of the paradox about the stagnation of the indicators of happiness), these trends in no way augur a transition towards a postmaterialist society.[4] 'Low cost' transportation and mass tourism today form part of the consumer society, in the same way that yesterday we bought cars. You have to earn a good living to acquire them! Leisure is everything – except free. The duration of working life has certainly dropped – for men especially. Yet if we take into account the evolution of female work, the hours worked at the end of the twentieth century are almost identical for an American household to what they were a century earlier. To judge from the difficulty the immense majority have in getting through the month without going broke, society seems quite far from the ideal of saturation of material needs that economic growth had seemed to promise. Immediate consumption constantly encounters insurmountable obstacles.

Thus according to a French survey on living conditions, two persons out of three in France today feel they are imposing spending restrictions on themselves. The portion of 'constrained expenses' never stops rising; these are incompressible expenses that a household must confront (e.g. lodging, water, electricity and taxes, but also insurance, school cafeterias, television . . .). Housing, which is the largest item, constantly costs more, since it almost mechanically accompanies the rise in average income. Since everyone must flee relegation to the lower levels of society, this makes it ever more expensive to find housing in 'good neighbourhoods'. For others, the costs of transport always grow in proportion to the distance necessary to travel to find cheaper real estate. In total, the portion of the combination 'housing plus transport' has gone in fifty years from 27 per cent to 36 per cent of overall expenses in France. For the poorest 20 per cent, all the constrained expenses, according to the French statistical institute INSEE, amount to three-quarters of their disposable income. The ten per cent at the bottom of the ladder are left at the end of the month with only a few dozen euros at best.

The promise of a postmaterialist society was first announced a long while ago, and it still seems vain. In the middle of the nineteenth century, it appeared from the pen of John Stuart Mill, the celebrated British economist and philosopher. For him, economic growth was a flash in the pan and destined to trail off. He gave the name 'stationary state' to the ineluctable point where material growth is interrupted.

> It is scarcely necessary to remark that a stationary condition of capital and population implies a stationary state of human improvement. There would be as much scope as ever for all kinds of mental culture, and more social progress, as much room for improving the Art of Living, and much more likelihood of its being improved, when minds cease to be engrossed by the art of getting on.

In other words, people will no longer be concerned to get richer when growth has disappeared.[5]

The vision of a Communist society elaborated by Marx and Engels is likewise animated by the idea that the forces of production will one day permit each person to be given according to his needs – but these needs outstrip the capacity to satisfy them. Another famous economist, J. M. Keynes, also promised that one day humans would become sufficiently better-off and would only have to worry about 'true problems': living nicely, human relationships, creation – in short, the last stages of Maslow's pyramid.

> The course of affairs will simply be that there will be ever larger and larger classes and groups of people for whom problems of economic necessity have been practically removed . . . Meanwhile there will be no harm in making mild preparation for our destiny, in encouraging and experimenting in the arts of life, as well as the activities of purpose.[6]

Keynes hailed economists as guardians 'not of civilization, but the possibility of civilization', to the extent that they are able to accelerate the advent of this outcome.

More recently, a sociologist called Ronald Inglehart states that he can discern the premises of a postmaterialist society.[7] In the studies he has analysed, a growing number of interviewees mention projects of 'self-realization' as important to them. But the answers do not commit the interviewees themselves to do anything, but rather reflect the type of society they think is desirable. In their most direct response to the question of what would make them happier, 70 per cent respond: a higher income. In the United States, as in all 'rich' countries, 'materialist' aspirations have by no means diminished over time.

In fact everything shows that economic growth, as we have known it for two centuries, simply cannot bear within in itself the conditions for its disappearance. The economic system tries to preserve itself by constantly renewing the material needs that need to be satisfied and by (scientifically) sharpening the social rivalry among potential consumers. A want is incessantly created among those who otherwise would remain left out.

Analysing poverty, Amartya Sen observed that a poor person without access to television is deprived not of a superfluous good, but of an essential dimension of his life: that of sharing the same imaginary world as his fellow creatures.[8] To say that modern poverty is 'relative' does not change anything about the situation. Of course, television did not exist a hundred years ago, but now that it is here, to deprive poor people of TV would constitute a real privation for them. Today the mobile phone, unknown ten years ago, has become an essential ingredient of ordinary life. Young people who do not have one suffer from exclusion from their friends' world. As Easterlin concludes, if we do not openly discuss the issue of what we call a 'good life', then we cannot become the masters of the kind of growth that we desire.

The Spectre of Marx

The idea of a postmaterialist society is one of the lost illusions of the postmodern world in the realm of consumption.

On the production side, the disillusionment is no less profound. Lyotard makes an explicit link between 'postmodernity' and the idea of a 'postindustrial' society as theorized by Daniel Bell and Alain Touraine, which marks the shift from a society based on working-class labour to a society where creation triumphs over production. In the new society of knowledge, the heroes are savants, the learned, the skilful. Difficult work on an assembly line comes to be replaced by the mildness of tertiary work in the service sector. However, as regards the work of cashiers, nurses, engineers, stock market traders, or scholars, the postindustrial world may be everything – whether unequal, exciting or repetitive – *except* gentle and peaceful.

The specific problem of tertiary work relates to the fact that it possesses weak productivity reserves. Many writers have stressed that growth in the services was of a totally different kind from that recorded in industry or agriculture.[9] A haircut or theatre play, today like yesterday, takes the same amount of time to be accomplished. The gains in productivity due to technology are meagre, even nil. Consequently, economic growth and salary progress are both doomed to remain weak. It does not matter that service sector employees might initially be better paid than workers in industry (which, moreover, is not always the case, especially to the extent that union power is weaker in the former). What is lost is any growth in pay.

Thus to obtain a rise in income when growth is unattainable, each person must redouble his or her effort. Here the computer revolution is going to play a decisive role, since it brings to the service sector the levers of growth that electricity once brought to the industrial sector. As the 'all-digital' replaced the 'all-electric', the 1990s saw a gradual inflection of ideas about stagnation in tertiary productivity. This was the period when distribution, for example, became 'high-tech' thanks to bar-codes, logistics and stock management in real time.[10] But the way in which productivity has been increased has poured cold water on the hopes of a society that wants to free itself from the harshness of the industrial world.

It has become customary to speak of a third industrial revolution to characterize the digital revolution, taking its place after the steam revolution in the eighteenth century and the electrical in the nineteenth century. Yet the digital revolution is quite different from its two predecessors. This is not an energy revolution; it does not change the technology that would enable doing a job like cutting hair any faster by operating a machine. It does not reduce the time necessary to read a book, see a film, read a message . . . It is a revolution in the management of information, a managerial revolution that is overthrowing techniques of organizing work.

As Philippe Askenazy shows perfectly well, 'digital productivity' increases in a firm only when it is accompanied by a re-organization of work.[11] This makes it possible to require a worker to perform several tasks at once, to fight downtime 'scientifically'. The office worker who types his own texts, the bank employee who accomplishes alone tasks previously devolved on several people, the night watchman who does the next day's accounts – are all examples of this phenomenon. Gains in productivity do then emerge, but they derive from a crucial factor: the intensification of work. A reduction in costs – 'cost-cutting' – has become the key. A 'neo-Stakhanovism' is put in place that aims to increase the number of 'useful' minutes per hour worked. The responsibility weighing on the worker is by no means reduced by computers, which instead appear as a factor of multi-tasking and stress.

Is 'cost-cutting' sufficient to generate rapid growth? Speculating on the prospects for the next twenty years, Robert Gordon,[12] the great specialist in the subject, prudently concludes that the record growth formerly achieved when the electric revolution took off will probably *not* be reproduced by the digital revolution.[13] While productivity growth rose to almost five per cent during the years from 1920 to 1950 in the United States, he foresees a much more modest growth of two per cent over the next twenty years. This is a lot at the level of history, but remember that we have to deduct the rising cost of raw materials and of essential 'investments' in goods like education and health.[14]

By all accounts, the 'neo-Stakhanovist' nature of the expected growth explains why Marx's analyses concerning the exploitation of workers and the search for labour surplus suddenly seem relevant in the postindustrial era. It is indeed the intensification of work that becomes the principal vector of gains in productivity. Far from liberating us from the constraints of production, postindustrial society exacerbates them.

Healthy Expenditures

The hope that postindustrial society might furnish a break with the past has been disappointed, from the standpoints of both postmaterialist aspirations and conditions of production. Nevertheless, very visible modifications in the structure of employment have been produced in the course of the last fifty years. Among the standards of postindustrial society pre-eminently stand education, research, health and the digital economy. But the problem of these sectors is that they all have difficulty entering into the framework of the market economy. In a paradoxical way, given the needs to which they correspond, they appear either as costs or as perturbations in the economy, lacking a true 'business model'.

As we saw earlier, Robert Boyer has described an 'anthropogenic' revolution as characterizing the new frontiers of economic growth. The evolution in employment towards health and education testifies to a process in which humans are both instrument and substance matter of the new economic growth. One of the principal consequences of extending longevity over the last fifty years has been to extend the duration of studies as well![15]

But education, like health, is not among the usual categories of merchandise. The public sector plays a considerable role in every nation. Education is a passport for life, but it also reproduces even more cruelly the inequalities of birth. Nobody would accept education being left to market forces alone. The countries where education performs best, according to the studies conducted by the OECD (PISA), are certainly not the ones where the portion of private expenditure is highest. Finland, champion of the world in educational success, owes this achievement principally to an innovative pedagogy that is animated by a concern for the success of everybody. Competition among students and among schools is not the recipe for educational success.[16]

Scientific research, which generally takes place in establishments of higher education, is certainly subject to worldwide competition, but 'knowledge' does not reside in the fields of the market economy. Ideas need to circulate freely in order to prosper. In fact, basic research provides an excellent model of an activity that succeeds in being both competitive and cooperative at the same time. Progress in knowledge is spectacular, and will perhaps displace the frontiers of humanity. It will enable the private sector to prosper, but only down the line. The market is nourished by a flow of knowledge whose logic of creation always escapes that market's comprehension.

Health is another striking example. In the United States, health expenditure has reached 17 per cent of total GDP! In France, it has reached 11 per cent, but in 1960 it represented less than four per cent. Brigitte Dormont has shown that this rise relates essentially to progress in medicine.[17] It is not a by-product of an ageing population, but comes from innovations (sometimes radical) that increase the social demand for health services. It has become common to speak of health costs spiralling 'out of control'. But could you say that car sales also soar due to 'out of control' motorists? Why on earth should one want to reduce this particular evolution?

Health is not a product like others. It does not enter into the classic scheme of supply and demand, for which fixing a price ensures equilibrium. It requires close regulation of the health professions, and public or private insurance to protect clients. More than any other sector, it depends on progress in the branch of medical research, which is by nature a public good. Just as one would not tolerate first-class passengers being the only ones to have parachutes, it would be unacceptable if a vaccine against AIDS benefited only those who had the means to buy it.

The digital economy is the other factor that has revolutionized the conditions of production. But it, too, has much difficulty finding its own business model. The Internet destroys value, especially in the press, publishing, and music. Except for the giants like Google or Facebook, it is hard to make money on the Internet. The digital economy is dependent to a great extent on the objects that serve as their platforms – tablets and smartphones – and on the advertising they manage to hijack. Facebook, which is a link that is pure and free between its users, is always looking for sources of revenue in proportion to the number of Web surfers that pass through. Right now, the firm brings back less than three euros per year per user, which explains the disappointing share price when Facebook was introduced on the stock market. The only way of existing financially is to hijack (sometimes by hacking into) a share of the traffic for advertising classic goods. For example, Clara is organizing her birthday party in the country when she receives (without asking for it) advertising for BBQ sauces!

The financial promise of new Internet giants relates to their capacity to drain off the advertising for toothpaste and spaghetti. The digital economy cannot stand on its own, any more than could the Roman Empire, as we recall from Schiavone . . .

A 'digital communism' sometimes figures as a new utopia that will come along to resolve these contradictions. Richard Barbrook writes about how entrepreneurs and hackers argued over whether the Web was e-commerce or a gift economy. 'Within this virtual community, the gift economy was in ascendancy over the market economy.'[18] Gratuitousness makes some people grit their teeth. Obviously, artists do not appreciate it this way, since they are resolved to defend their right (moral and financial) to be remunerated for their work. How could they live as artists if their works were given away? Studying the careers of musicians, Maya Beauvallet shows that their income has not dropped on average in the course of the last thirty years.[19] The rise in concert sales figures has enabled a compensation for the collapse of sales receipts linked to the sale of records and CDs. We cannot take up this now-classic debate, but it puts a finger on the major contradiction in the digital economy. While it destroys value in its own world (digital music), it gives its operators a living – but only in proportion to the other activities it allows to be generated. It must recover the materiality of the world (live shows, advertising) in order to exist.

Here again, as with health, capitalism struggles because new social needs do not fit into the traditional logic of market goods. Marx spoke of a contradiction between the productive forces and relations of production. He meant that the wealth created by capitalism remained contingent on the framework of private property, which was itself too narrow. In the era of the Internet, many observers have made the same diagnosis.

Returning to Happiness

The difficulty of measuring in monetary units the full reality of the postindustrial economy leads some people to want to measure it otherwise than in euros or dollars. For example, some attempts at virtual currencies have already been tried. In the video game 'Second Life', where each person can live a second life via an avatar, the 'linden dollar' is the currency in circulation, which allows buying and selling all sorts of virtual activities, ranging from producing shows to prostitution (also virtual).

We may go beyond this and imagine that Google one day creates a central bank that issues a new monetary unit with which one can buy and sell the right to see videos or read blogs. Each Gmail account would have an endowment of a thousand I-money, like in Monopoly. This money would enable access to all the offers in the digital world. The classic problems of money would arise, of course: avoiding inflation, preventing counterfeiting, convertibility into other currencies (like yahoo-money). But monetary history shows that none of these problems is insurmountable. Conversion into true dollars might take place on a market of floating exchanges. But as with Monopoly parties among friends, the tokens would count less for their real value than for the recognition they give to the players.

Here we may think of the debate that made Marx say that Proudhon was naive when he proposed abolishing capitalism by paying workers with vouchers indicating the number of hours they had worked. This controversy posed the same issue as today: if capitalism becomes too narrow a framework to support the full development of productive forces, what other solutions are available?

If we forego measuring wealth numerically (actually or virtually), might one path be to calculate it in units of happiness? Such an approach would be audacious but not unreasonable. Economists who specialize in happiness (whose work I have drawn on throughout this book) have demonstrated in a convincing way that the indices they use have an indisputable scientific strength, for example by enabling a prediction about whether a couple will divorce or whether an individual will commit suicide. Doesn't happiness offer a more useful criterion for public policies than the 'wealth' produced?

For many people, the question seems a provocation. Happiness is subjective, so how could it be made into an objective indicator? The GDP, which measures the national revenue in euros or dollars, has the principal merit (despite its weaknesses) of being able to be calculable.[20] Moreover, from the standpoint of people's needs, as we have seen, the idea of a postmaterialist society seems quite remote from the reality experienced by most of them. What does aiming for the happiness of the greatest number mean when 70 per cent of the persons questioned respond that they quite simply want a higher income? Would policymakers follow an index of happiness that would run against the wishes of the interested parties? Evidently that would be a contradiction in terms. 'I want to be happy, but I live with people who want to be happy too,' said Diderot in his Encyclopedia article on 'Society'. We cannot decide about people's wellbeing without taking into account the judgements they make of their own actions. But at the same time, their own judgement might be constantly distorted, including from the retrospective viewpoint that they will one day have. And even if the poorest have adjusted to the worst, why should we leave them to their fate?[21] Happiness is quickly transformed into a trap if it is taken literally.

Nobody better than Amartya Sen has put a finger on the difficulties to be resolved. To grasp the logic of his reasoning, let us take the following example, inspired by one that he has offered. Suppose that Kim has decided to spend the day at home, reading or watching television, waiting for his wife to come home in the evening. But imagine that he discovers suddenly that his wife, in leaving in the morning, has locked him into their apartment. So he has no option but to wait for her to come back. The result seems exactly identical to the one he had planned to do: to stay at home and wait for his wife. From an 'economic' point of view, that is fine. Yet everything has changed for Kim. His own plan has been transformed into a necessity. He is stifling in a life that he himself chose. Being shut up in an identity, Kim is the victim of claustrophobia of a metaphysical kind, which relates to the fact that he is being denied the right to be in disagreement with himself. It is one thing for Kim to wish to shut himself in his apartment, and quite another thing for this to be imposed on him.

This example illustrates the way in which Sen criticizes the strictly economic approach to happiness. Economists, he explains, are 'consequentialists': they judge a tree only by its fruits. If Kim prefers A to B, one gains time and money by eliminating B and only offering him A . . . But by wanting to rationalize the world, one shuts it in a 'steel cage', as the sociologist Max Weber said. One amputates from life a crucial dimension: freedom of choice.

Starting from this analysis, Sen assigns to public policies a goal that is modest in appearance, which is to give each person the 'capability' of living a life worthy of his or her expectations. 'Capability' – a term forged from 'capacity' and 'ability' – signifies that people should be endowed with resources that permit them to live as they wish. This is a philosophy that invites grasping the real freedom to choose between different ways of leading one's life. That of a poor person is not necessarily less interesting than that of a rich person, but the question should be whether the person who adopts that way of life really chose to do so. If circumstances decided for him or her that there is justification for offering a wider choice, this augments capacities to act, even if in the end the person makes the same choice, or if – worse – the other path would *de facto* reduce the person's happiness.

Starting from life as people wish to lead it does not imply a neo-liberalism that, in another form, would amount to letting them sort themselves out on their own. People no longer go to live opera very much, and this is certainly a loss from the viewpoint of opera-lovers. But the question that must be asked is whether this is their choice – the opera does not interest anybody in the age of the Internet – or because there are no longer ways of learning about opera to bring them to it.[22] The analysis of poverty by Banerjee and Duflo shows how much the supposed freedom of choice is transformed into slavery if it is not constantly supported by the institutions that aid everybody to be lifted above their immediate needs. A just society and a just policy must find on the razor's edge a balance that verifies that the formal rights – to education and to culture – are 'really' transformed into the freedom to live the lives people actually wish for.[23]

This approach will not magically solve fundamental questions: Are we heading today, individually and collectively, towards an impasse, notably that of a materialist society that does not keep – and will never keep – its promises? In a phrase from the anthropologist Marshall Sahlins, it is possible that 'we are condemning ourselves to forced labour in perpetuity', while being haunted by the opposite idea, that we will soon escape it.[24] But there exists no other means to decide such questions than to debate them democratically, by opening up the right to social experimentation and by taking into account the relevant research to augment our knowledge of the world and of its real possibilities.

As Laurence Fontaine well summarizes it, Sen's thinking in this domain is both modest and ambitious: modest because it prefers partial advances to the desire to create a perfectly just society, and also because it is aware of all the non-fulfilments, starting with those born of human complexity [. . .] But it is also magnificently ambitious in its constant desire to place at the centre of things each man and each woman, not just in his or her humanity (championed in the ethical framework of human rights and as an actor – not just the receptacle of various objects of comfort) but also as human beings whose freedom to live the lives they want to lead must be respected and strengthened.[25]

Conclusion

The Chinese novelist Yu Hua explained that the political repression in Tiananmen Square provided the real lift-off for Chinese economic growth. With the democratic road blocked, the Chinese would now seek in wealth an ersatz satisfaction for their forbidden passions. Yu Hua finds here a rationale that was also maintained in the eighteenth century in order to justify the place offered to the economy. At that time, the desire for wealth was similarly considered to be a vice among others, a variant of vanity, self-love and lust.

However, as the economist and philosopher Albert Hirschman explains,[1] the desire for wealth must nevertheless be distinct from other passions, since it is interpreted by moralists and economists themselves as a 'compensatory passion', meaning a passion that appeases and sometimes extinguishes the others. For Jean-Pierre Dupuy, who adopts this interpretation, the economy in this sense has assumed the place of the sacred, in that it is summoned to 'contain' human violence, in both senses of the word, i.e. preventing it and containing it (as in a sack).[2]

This theory of 'compensatory passion' has proved to be quite fragile at the level of history. The twentieth century succeeded in the *tour de force* of being both the most prosperous and the most barbarous. From the standpoint of technological innovations, the millennial century that just opened has roared off, like the previous one. The all-digital replaces the all-electric, and other evolutions are taking shape, those of genetics and renewable energy sources. Whether the all-digital has the power to entrain the whole economy in new technologies remains uncertain, however. It seems improbable that it will enable matching – or even approaching – the industrial growth of the twentieth century. If we take into account the hike in prices of raw materials that will cut into the buying power of the importing countries for a long while, and the cost of the investments represented by health and education, then the 'compensatory passion' will be feeble, at least in the advanced countries.

Faced with these immense transformations, Homo Economicus is a poor prophet. Wanting to overcome the obstacles that blocked the pursuit of enrichment and in the name of efficiency, he chased away his own competitors, Homo Ethicus, Homo Empathicus – the other aspects of a human being that aspire to cooperation and reciprocity. But by triumphing over his rivals, he is in fact dying, shutting human nature up in a world devoid of any ideal – and this ultimately ineffective.

Humans do possess a formidable capacity of adaptation. Their obsession with comparing themselves to others allows them to go almost anywhere – provided that others go there, too. But thinking that competition will suffice to organize the coming world derives from an anthropological illusion that would be costly if it were not mitigated by other 'compensatory passions'. In the balance between competition and cooperation, we have to reanimate the latter, by restoring the enchantment of work, by dismantling the boundaries between the free and the paid for and by rethinking international cooperation (starting with that within Europe). In its time, Christianity offered a solution to the crisis of the Roman Empire, liberating ancient people from the complexities of a society that had become unintelligible. In our turn, we must think again about the idea we nurture of a world in harmony with itself, that it may lead us to feel 'the fore-taste of happiness and peace'.

Notes

Introduction

1 Jean-Claude Ameisen, *Sur les Epaules de Darwin: Les Battements du Temps* (*On Darwin's Shoulders*) (Editions les Liens qui Libèrent, 2012).

1 Gross Domestic Happiness

1 Cathy Scott-Clark and Adrian Levy, 'Fast Forward into Trouble', *Guardian*, 14 June 2003. Bhutan's king became famous for totally banning cigarettes. The kingdom was one of the poorest in the world according to the United Nations' measures of human development. Also quoted by Richard Layard, *Happiness: Lessons from a New Science* (Penguin, 2006).

2 Robert Putnam, *Bowling Alone: The Collapse and Revival of American Community* (Simon & Schuster, 2000), p. 241.

3 Forty per cent of adults and 70 per cent of adolescents recognize that they are watching too much television. It is evidently possible that the causality is the reverse: unhappy people who are unable to face life watch too much television. But several control experiments have shown that the causality runs from television to unhappiness.

4 S. M. McClue, D. I. Laibson, G. Loewenstein, D. Cohen, 'Separate Neural Systems Value Immediate and Delayed Monetary Rewards', *Science*, 2004.

5 Fabrice Etile, 'La Grande Bouffe', CEPREMAP, 2012, Editions rue d'Ulm; Claudia Senik, 'Peut-on dire que les Français sont malheureux?' in *16 Nouvelles questions d'économie contemporaine* (Albin Michel, 2010).

6 Bruno Frey, *Happiness: A Revolution in Economics* (MIT Press, 2008).

7 Daniel Kahneman has shown that the psychological cost of a colonoscopy can be reduced by leaving the patient longer in the operating room after the procedure. The last memory becomes the less painful one.

8 Boris Cyulnik has written about people's formidable resilience in the face of personal tragedies.

9 The explanatory variables of American happiness are almost identical to those that account for European happiness. See R. Di Tella and R. MacCulloch, 'Gross National Happiness as an Answer to the Eastern Paradox', *National Bureau of Economic Research*, 86 (2008). Nevertheless, according to the Gallup Institute, the number of Americans who declare themselves to be 'very happy' fell by a third between 1956 and 2006. It is stable in Europe.

10 George Loewenstein, Ted O'Donoghue and Matt Rabin called this attitude 'projection bias'. See *Quarterly Journal of Economics*, 1 November 2003.

11 Kant adds that 'the concept of happiness is so indeterminate a concept that even though every human being wishes to achieve it, yet he can never say determinately and in agreement with himself what he actually wishes and wants'. *Kant: Groundwork to the Metaphysics of Morals*, trans. Mary Gregor and Jens Timmerman (Cambridge University Press, 2012), pp. 31–2.

12 Rabelais, *Gargantua*, book 34, trans. Thomas Urquhart and Peter Motteux (Simon and Brown, 2013), quoted by Thierry Pech, *Le Temps des riches* (Paris: Le Seuil, 2011).

13 Gary Becker and Richard Posner, *Uncommon Sense: Economic Insights from Marriage to Terrorism* (Chicago, 2009).

14 Jeremy Bentham, *An Introduction to the Principles of Morals and Legislation* (White Dog, 2010).

15 Epicurean happiness is negatively defined as 'apony', which signifies the absence of pain, and positively defined as 'ataraxy', which signifies the absence of trouble in a soul, defined as the prudent regulation of all desires.

16 Aristotle, *Nichomachean Ethics*, trans. Terence Irwin, Book I, ch. 8.

17 Andre Comte-Sponville, *Le Capitalisme est-il moral?* (Paris: Albin Michel, 2004).

18 Jon Elster, 'Ulysses and the Siren', in *Ulysses Unbound* (Cambridge University Press, 2000).

19 David Laibson indicates that experiments with pigeons reveal the same trope.

20 Bruno Frey, *Happiness: A Revolution in Economics*, op. cit.

2   Work: A Diminishing Value

1 On these points see Chad Syverson's article, 'What determines Productivity?' *Journal of Economic Literature*, June 2011.

2 The sociologist Vilfredo Pareto said, 'One makes the same mistake when one accuses political economy of not taking morality into account; this is like accusing a chess theory of not taking culinary arts into account.' *Manuel d'économie politique* (1906) (Droc, 1966), quoted by Christian Laval, *L'Homme économique* (Paris: Gallimard, 2007).

3 Pierre-Yves Gome, 'La Source de la contre-productivité', *Le Monde*, 17 January 2012, finds that the quality of the welcome in a supermarket depends prosaically on the natural empathy of the cashiers towards the customers. Yet performance norms put considerable stress on checkout personnel. Thus equality and loyalty deteriorate, and management reacts by offering the consumer various kinds of loyalty cards to the chain, which it is up to the cashiers to administer, increasing their duties and constraints. Ivan Illych invented the concept of 'counter-productivity' to explain why systems of government become inefficient.

4 See Yann Algan, Pierre Cahuc and Andre Zylberberg, *La Fabrique de la défiance* (Paris: Albin Michel, 2012), which shows that the French do not achieve good results in the 'trust game'.
5 It is obvious that humans need to feel a tie with other people. One of the constant characteristics of happiness is an ability to trust others. The French are on average less happy, in large part because they suffer from a lack of systematic trust in others. But in the United States, too, the percentage of Americans who declare that they have trust in others has fallen from 56 per cent in the 1960s to 33 per cent today.
6 The work of Matt Rabin shows how to revisit game theory on the basis of these notions. See also Jon Elster, *Le Désinteressement* [volume 1 of a trilogy on economic man] (Paris: Le Seuil, 2009).
7 Laurence Fontaine, in *L'Economie morale* (Paris: Gallimard, 2008) illustrates the logic at work by analysing the 'pre-economic' ties that were still apparent in the seventeenth century.
8 In *Les Stratégies absurdes* (Paris: Le Seuil, 2010).
9 But when the system was dismantled, parents continued to arrive late, with the same frequency as under the 'penalty' system, more often than at the start of the experiment. Uri Gneezy and Aldo Rusticini, 'A Fine is a Price', *Journal of Legal Studies*, January 2000.
10 Roland Benabou and Jean Tirole, 'Belief in a Just World and Redistributive Politics', *Quarterly Journal of Economics*, MIT Press, 121 (2) May 2006, pp. 699–746.
11 In her book *Les Stratégies absurdes*, op. cit.
12 An immense literature has developed to analyse these mutations. The roles of new technologies and of globalization have been weighed and calibrated. The classic explanation of the rise of American inequalities is supposed to relate to a 'rise in the return on education'. In 1980, a graduate of higher education earned 40 per cent more (on average) than a high-school graduate. In 2005, he earned 90 per cent more on average. The collapse of trade unions played a more direct role, as witnessed (for example) by a comparison with Canada, where the same technological discontinuities were observed without a corresponding rise in inequalities. Another explanation is immigra-

tion. Migrants represented only five per cent of the American population in 1970, but since then they have risen to about 15 per cent, the level reached in 1910. But according to Borjas and Kalz, this has reduced the salaries of non-college graduates by only five per cent.

13 Cullen Murphy, *Are We Rome? The Fall of an Empire and the Fate of America* (Houghton Mifflin, 2007), p. 16.

14 The rise in inequality in France does not have the same scope as in the United States. The Cotis Report (2009), relying on the work of Camille Landais and Thomas Piketty, shows that while in France the highest income bracket records spectacular growth rates, the macroeconomic effect remains more limited (without being negligible).

15 On all these points, see Jonathan Heathcote, Fabrizio Perri and Giovanni L. Violante, 'Unequal We Stand: An Empirical Analysis of Economic Inequality in the United States 1967–2006', *National Bureau of Economic Research*, 15483, 2009.

16 Thomas Piketty and Emmanuel Saez, 'Income Inequality in the United States 1913–1998', *Quarterly Journal of Economics*, 118 (1) 2003. See also http://else.berkely.edu/-saex/Tab FIG2010.XLS

17 The French figures are as follows: The median level that exactly divides the French population into two equal parts is about 1,500 euros a month. To enter into the top ten per cent, you have to earn more than 3,000 euros; into the top five per cent, more than 5,500 euros; into the top one per cent, more than 10,000 euros. To enter into the stratosphere of the ultra-rich, the top 0.01 per cent – the highest ten-thousandth – you have to earn the famous million a year. At the time 6,000 French people qualified as ultra-rich. France is well represented in the hit parade of wealth. With only one per cent of the world population, it includes about ten per cent of the millionaires. I take these figures and those that follow from Thierry Pech, *Le Temps des riches*, op. cit.

18 Olivier has analysed the sector deformation that was produced over time. In 1976, 36 per cent of the working rich came from industry. Finance represented only six per cent of these millionaires, and other services to enterprises, 14 per cent of them.

In 2007, industrialists belonging to the club of the ultra-rich represented more than 14 per cent of the members, services to companies 27 per cent and financiers 24 per cent.

19 The author of these lines has had the personal experience of misunderstandings born of the idea of the 'working rich' by trying to explain it in a radio programme where he had to make a child aged eight understand why there were rich people and poor people. He was later reproached for wanting to prove that inequalities were natural!

20 Lucian Bebchuk and Jesse Fried, *Pay without Performance* (Cambridge MA: Harvard University Press, 2004). Several scandals have surfaced, like stock options backdated to optimize their return.

21 Xavier Gabaix and Augustin Landier in 'Why has CEO Pay Increased So Much?' (*Quarterly Journal of Economics*, 123 (1), 2008), analyse negotiations over CEO pay through the prism of Becker's marriage theory. The 'couple' formed by the company and the boss is subject to dual bargaining: the former says, 'I have other candidates', and the latter says, 'I can go elsewhere.' In the end, bosses extract their pay relative to their supposed rarity. This pay is actually rather low (according to Gabaix and Landier), amounting to less than 0.02 per cent of the company's capitalization. (Another author, Marko Tervio, finds higher figures, but the reasoning is the same.) However, related to total capital, bosses earn several millions. According to this theory, only the relative scale of remuneration remains important. Taxing bosses uniformly would not change anything in the equilibrium.

22 Robert Frank, *Richistan: A Journey through the American Wealth Boom and the Lives of the New Rich* (New York: Crown, 2007), pp. 3–4.

23 This process has already been seen in history. The Reformation represented a 'lowering' of the cultural summits reached in the Middle Ages by Michelangelo, Montaigne and Shakespeare. Today, one speaks of a 'lowering' of the summits reached by the 'high culture' of the nineteenth and twentieth centuries. See Perry Anderson, *The Origins of Postmodernity* (London: Verso, 1998).

3 The Decline of Empire

1 Undoubtedly the age of Marcus Aurelius was the golden age of the Roman Empire, according to Edward Gibbon, who wrote in the eighteenth century the classic *Decline and Fall of the Roman Empire*.

2 In *The Making of Late Antiquity* (Harvard University Press, 1972), Peter Brown challenged the 'magnificently personal and brilliant' view of Mikhail Rostovtzeff, who found an 'embourgeoisement' of ancient Rome as the cause of its troubles.

3 Peter Brown, ibid. See also his *Through the Eye of the Needle: Wealth, the Fall of Rome, and the Making of Christianity in the West, 350–550* (Princeton University Press, 2012).

4 Brown, op cit., pp. 34–5. Doing so, the benefactor earned the right to 'make oracles speak'.

5 Ibid., p. 46.

6 Ibid., p. 47. Roman inequalities were much more radical than those today in the United States. The Roman elite (1.5 per cent of the population) captured 20 per cent of the total wealth; the following group (10 per cent of the population) also received 20 per cent, which is not too remote from the contemporary American situation. But thereafter the difference is stark: the remaining 80 per cent of Romans lived on the poverty threshold. An 'average' plebeian was poor. There was no 'middle class' in Rome.

7 Quoted in Aldo Schiavone, *The End of the Past: Ancient Rome and the Modern West*, trans. Margery Schneider (Cambridge MA: Harvard University Press, 2000), p. 7.

8 Ibid., p. 25.

9 J.-M. Carrie and A. Rousselle, 'L'Empire romain en mutation, de Sévères à Constantin, 192–337', *Nouvelle Histoire de l'Antiquité*, 10 (Paris: Seuil 'Points d'Histoire', 1999).

10 The tax system of the Lower Empire established by Diocletian and affirmed by Constantine relied on a personal tax (the *capitatio*) and a property tax (the *jugatio*).

11 Alessandro Barbero, *The Day of the Barbarians: The Battle that Led to the Fall of the Roman Empire*, trans. John Cullen (Walker, 2007).

12 Paul Veyne, *Quand notre monde est devenu Chrétien* (Paris: Albin Michel, 2007), *When Our World Became Christian*, trans. Jane Lloyd (Polity, 2010).

13 Brown, op. cit., p. 59.

14 Paul Veyne, op. cit. This is the period when the practice of making wills arose: 'Between the individual and his wealth, whatever its form – patrimony or acquisitions, real estate or movable property – the line was now direct and exclusive. Each asset belonged to some person.'

15 Jean-Pierre Vernant, 'The Individual within the City-State', in *Mortals and Immortals: Collected Essays* (Princeton, 1991). Louis Dumont, *Essais sur l'individualisme* (Paris: Seuil, 1991).

16 Charles Kahn, 'The Total Lack of the Cartesian Sense of a Radical and Necessary Incompatibility between Thought and Awareness on the One Hand, and Physical Extension on the Other', *Sensation and Consciousness in Aristotle's Psychology*, Archiv fur Geschichte der Philosophie, 48 (1–3), pp. 43–81, quoted by Jean-Pierre Vernant, 'The Individual within the City-State', op. cit.

17 Aristotle, *Politics*, trans. William Ellis, Book I ch. 2.

18 Paul Veyne, op. cit.

19 For example, Cullen Murphy, *Are we Rome? The Fall of an Empire and the Fate of America* (2007), trans. Arthur goldhammer, pp. 625, 627.

20 George Bush, Press Conference, 14 April 2003.

21 Alexis de Tocqueville, *Democracy in America*, vol. 2, ch. 13.

22 Alesina, Glaeser, Sacerdote, 'Why Doesn't the US have a European-Style Welfare State?' (2001). http://papers.ssrn.com/sol3/papers.cfm?abstract_id=290047

23 Commenting on how the United States labour market works, the economic historian Stanford Gavin Wright showed that American distrust of 'labour contracts' should be understood in reference to the need to finally turn the page on slavery.

Thus any contract of long duration is suspect, since it evokes a link with a slave's indefinite subordination.

24 Robert Putnam, *Bowling Alone: The Collapse and Revival of American Community*, op. cit.
25 Ibid., p. 89.
26 Ibid., p. 90.
27 As Julia Cage has shown, the impoverishment of the serious press (whatever the causes, such as competition from the Internet) explains the inroads of 'trash' press, which is less expensive to produce (than serious investigative reporting) and still draws readers' attention.
28 Quoted in Putnam, ibid., p. 217.
29 Robert Wuthrow, quoted in Putnam, p. 152.
30 Vaclav Smil, *Why America is Not a New Rome* (MIT Press, 2010).
31 By some estimates, more than half the growth comes from the spill-over from innovations. In a famous joke, Steve Jobs reproached Bill Gates for having stolen the mouse from him and the idea for Windows. Bill answered him that they were both stolen from Xerox, and Steve did it first. Quoted by Stephen Cohen and Brad DeLong, *The Loss of Influence* (University of California Press, 2010).
32 Cited by *Les Echos*, 28 November 2011.
33 The ensemble formed by China, India and South Korea represents 46 per cent of the total, with 22 per cent Chinese students. The French, British and Germans send abroad somewhat fewer than 10,000 students. Overall, the United States has 75 per cent foreign students, the United Kingdom 8.5, Canada and Australia 5 per cent and 3 per cent respectively. France has only 1.4 per cent and Germany 1 per cent.

4   De-Centring the World

1 Aldo Schiavone, *Histoire et destin* (Belin, 2009).
2 Quoted in Stephen Cohen and Brad DeLong, *The End of Influence: What Happens When Other Countries Have the Money* (Basic Books, 2010), p. 62.

3 The number of countries with intermediate income, whose rates of growth are less than twice as high as rich countries, has been reduced by half (from 67 to 38) and 'poor countries' that do not record sufficient growth have dropped from 55 to 25. See the report from the Organization for Economic Cooperation and Development (OECD) 'Shifting Wealth', 2010.

4 Abijit Banerjee and Esther Duflo, *Repenser la pauvreté* (Paris: Le Seuil, 2011).

5 George Marshall was the US Secretary of State who launched a plan to help Europe and Japan after the Second World War.

6 Esther Duflo, *Poor Economics: A Radical Rethinking of the Way to Fight Global Poverty* (Public Affairs, 2011).

7 R. Hausmann, R. Rodriguez, R. Wagner, 'Growth Collapses', *CID Working Paper*, 136, Harvard, 2006.

8 Gunnar Myrdal, *Asian Drama: An Inquiry into the Poverty of Nations*, 1968.

9 Morishima, *Why Has Japan 'Succeeded'?: Western Technology and the Japanese Ethos* (Cambridge University Press, 1984).

10 Asia educated itself, and primary schooling is turning at 120 per cent. Secondary schooling went from 46 per cent to 76 per cent between 1980 and 2009. Access to higher education has increased nine-fold, to reach 19 per cent. In India, however, 40 per cent of the population is still illiterate.

11 Erik Izraelewicz was a journalist and economist who became director of *Le Monde*.

12 And still more, if we take into account the effect of its own growth on that of other countries. One point of Chinese growth might trigger between 0.2 and 0.4 growth points in poor or medium revenue countries.

13 Fareed Zakaria, *Post-American World* (New York: Norton, 2009), 2nd edn, 2012.

14 Yu Hua, *China in Ten Words*, trans. Allan H. Barr (New York: Pantheon, 2011), p. 159.

15 Lu Huilin, *Le Monde*, 4–5 Dec. 2011.

16 The world economic cycle tends to synchronize activity and employment with the indices of satisfaction. We find in Turkey,

South Africa and South Korea an evolution close to that registered in China, first a drop, then a rise to previous levels between the 1990s and 2000s, before the crisis.

17 'Goodbye Lenin (or not?): The Effect of Communism on People's Preferences', Alberto Alesina and Nichola Fuchs Schuendel, *National Bureau of Economic Research*, 1170 (October 2005).

18 Claudia Senik, taking up an idea of Albert Hirschman's, has called the mechanism of comparing oneself to others the 'tunnel effect' because it is similar to an automobile driver in a tunnel. Seeing the adjacent lane advance, he is at first pleased because he thinks the bottleneck is ending, then exasperated if his lane remains immobile.

19 Amartya Sen, 'More Than 100 Million Women are Missing', *NYRB*, 1990.

20 Robert Muchenbled, *A History of Violence from the End of the Middle Ages to the Present* (Cambridge: Polity, 2011).

21 Zhang Xiaobo, *Narratives of Chinese Economic Reforms*, (Textstream, 2010).

22 Yu Hua, op. cit., pp. 6, 19, 25.

23 Ibid., p. 113.

24 Ibid., p. 129.

25 Anatole Kaletsky, *Capitalism 4.0* (Public Affairs, 2010).

26 Lee Kuan Yew, *The Grand Master's Insights on China, the United States, and the World* (Cambridge MA: MIT Press, 2013).

27 Amartya Sen, *Development as Freedom* (Anchor, 2000), pp. 27, 234.

28 Ishac Diwan, 'A Rational Framework for the Understanding of the Arab Revolutions', Center for International Development, Harvard University, working paper 237, April 2012.

29 Robert Barro, 'Democracy and Growth', *NBER Working Paper*, 4909, 1994.

30 Demographics is one of the factors that has been upset by the diffusion of cultural models, especially through television. See for example *Soap Operas and Fertility* by Eliana La Ferrera et al., CEPR, 6785.

5   The Great Western Crisis

1 According to the statistics of Piketty and Saez, cited in Part II.
2 Charles Kindleberger, *Manias, Panics and Crashes: A History of Financial Crises* (Basic Books, 1981). A 'lender of last resort', usually a central bank or a creditor country, is an institution that has the means to furnish liquidity to banks or to nations that can no longer manage to finance themselves.
3 Milton Friedman and Anna Jacobson Schwartz, *A Monetary History of the United States, 1867–1960* (Princeton University Press, 1971).
4 Lilas Demmou, 'La Désindustrialisation en France', *DG Trésor*, June 2010.
5 Productivity gains destroy jobs but they also lower prices, which gives buying power to consumers. Calculated by volume – meaning fixing prices constant at their initial level – the share of industry in France's GDP is stable. Between 1997 and 2007, the share in volume of French industry was constant at 17 per cent of the total. In other words, according to this calculation, the decline of French industry is entirely explained by the decline in prices and not by the reduction of volume produced.
6 David Ricardo had conceived of the British strategy with the aid of the theory of 'comparative advantages'. England was a nation in advance of others, but still it won by specializing in the sector that possessed the highest potential. Ricardo thus pleaded for England to import foodstuffs, on condition that English peasants migrated to the dynamic sector, industry. The other countries obviously had to take the opposite road and specialize in sectors exporting raw materials (food or other), and then import English industrial products. This is why the countries concerned had spoken at the time of 'unequal exchange', reproaching England for keeping the best part for itself. Ricardo answered that they did not lose, since they could import less expensive products. The logic of 'comparative advantages' today remains a precious guide for understanding international commerce, even if it assumes very different

forms. A country like the United States subcontracts most of the manufacturing of its electronic products to Chinese enterprises. The most famous example is that of the Chinese firm Foxconn that makes Apple's smartphones. From the Chinese standpoint, this is a typical case of unequal exchange. For each iPhone sold at $459 by Apple, China earns $10; China claims it is the loser.

7 See, for example, Marc Melitz, 'The Impact of Trade on Intra-Industry Reallocations and Aggregate Industry Productivity', *Econometrica*, 2003; J. Eaton, S. Kortum, 'Technology, Geography, and Trade', *Econometrica* 70, 1741–79. These authors have noted that the firms that export are the most productive, which is not surprising. What is more surprising is that trade does not contribute to increasing their productivity, but merely gives them a larger playing field.

8 Philippe Chalmin, *Le Monde*, 17 January 2012.

9 www.swissre.com/sigma/

10 The problem with negative externalities is that nobody has an individual interest in avoiding them. It is difficult to capture profits from vaccines that take care of the poorest of the earth's population. The new generation of antibiotics is delayed, and for this reason investments are lagging behind. But they are indispensable in order to confront the new bacteria that are resistant to previous generations. Inversely, the over-use of antibiotics creates an externality: microbes get used to them (globally).

11 Michael Bordo and Barry Eichengreen, 'Crisis Now and Then', *NBER*, 8716, 2002.

12 During the last decade, a considerable effort was made by the World Health Organization to acquire a system of epidemiological surveillance, making it 'obligatory' to declare infections. Similarly, the 'Financial Stability Board' tried to anticipate global financial risks. Cyber risks, Internet viruses and cyber-criminality are other threats identified by the OECD that correlate with the growing interconnection of computers. The growing sophistication of computers will make it more and more difficult to detect viruses. In the course of the last ten years, cyber-criminality has been strongly professionalized.

The answer is primarily preventive, by storing data in back-up files.

6 Darwin's Nightmare

1 Robert Putnam, *Better Together: Restoring the American Community* (Simon & Schuster, 2004).
2 Marshall van Alstyne and Erik Brynjolfsson, 'Global Village or CyberBalkans: Modelling and Measuring the Integration of Electronic Communities', MIT Sloan School of Management, *NBER*, 2005.
3 Cybergeography.org
4 Antonio Casilli, *Les Liaisons numériques: vers une nouvelle sociabilité* (Paris: Le Seuil, 2010).
5 The speed of the transformations of which we are today the heirs is spectacular. In 1943, the first modern electronic calculator saw the light of day in the basement of a British base. It aimed to decode military communications. In 1951, a UNIVAC weighed 13 tonnes. Today, a child plays in his bedroom with an instrument that is many times more powerful. Cyberspace is the new frontier, to which we 'migrate' from the city. The number of Internet users has already topped two billion (http://www.internetworldstats.com/stats.htm).
6 Antonio Cassili, 'Culture numérique (Digital Culture)', *Communications*, 88, 2011.
7 Educated to move in a world of unlimited potentialities, young people lose a footing in the real world and seek to jettison their identity in favour of new ones, usually under a pseudonym.
8 *Issues in Social, Ethnic, and Cultural Research: 2011 Edition* (Google e-book).
9 Benabou and Tirole, 'Self Confidence and Personal Motivation', *Quarterly Journal of Economics*, August 2012.
10 On all these points, I allude to arguments in the book by Jean-Claude Ameisen, *Dans la Lumière et les Ombres: Darwin et le bouleversement du monde* (Paris: Editions Fayard/Editions du Seuil, October 2008).
11 Jean-Claude Ameisen, op. cit.

12 Francis Galton, *Essays in Eugenics* (Press of the Pacific, 2004).
13 See especially the excellent plea by Dominique Lestel, *L'Animal est l'avenir de l'homme* (Paris: Fayard, 2010).
14 See Katherine Pollard, 'What Makes Us Human?' *Scientific American*, May 2009.
15 Frans de Waal, *The Bonobo and the Atheist: In Search of Humanism Among the Primates* (Norton, 2013).
16 Giacomo Rizzolatti and Corrado Sinigaglia, *Mirrors in the Brain: How Our Minds Share Actions, Emotions, and Experience*, trans. Frances Anderson (Oxford University Press, 2008).
17 On this point, see Jean-Claude Ameisen, op. cit.
18 Studies of rats and mice show that calm parents may calm down agitated children (Wow!).
19 Francis Wolff, *Notre humanité, d'Aristote aux neurosciences* (Paris: Fayard, 2011).
20 On these points, listen to the fascinating debate between Alain Prochianz, biologist, and Philippe Descolla, anthropologist, called 'Is Man an Animal?' broadcast on France Culture, 30 July 2011. The biologist insisted on the break introduced by the appearance of Homo sapiens, whose cranial mass is much larger than it would be in an animal of the same size, while the anthropologist stressed a Western exceptionalism that always wants to make a radical separation between nature and culture.
21 Aldo Schiavone, *Histoire et destin*, op. cit.

7 The Postmodern Condition

1 Jean-François Lyotard, *The Postmodern Condition: A Report on Knowledge*, trans. Bennington and Massumi, 1984.
2 According to Debord, 'Reality erupts in the spectacle, and the spectacle is real . . . In the world that *really* has been turned on its head, truth is a moment of falsehood', *Society of the Spectacle*, pp. 8–9.

3 Rafaele Simone, 'Pourquoi l'Europe s'enracine à droite', *Le Monde*, 14 October 2010.

4 Richard Easterlin et. al, *Happiness, Growth and the Life Cycle* (Oxford University Press, 2011).

5 John Stuart Mill, *Principles of Political Economy*, Book IV, Chapter VI.

6 J. M. Keynes, 'Economic Possibilities for our Grandchildren' (1930), *Essays in Persuasion* (New York: Harcourt, 1974), p. 367.

7 Ronald Inglehart and Christian Weizel, *Modernization, Cultural Change and Democracy: The Human Development Sequence* (Cambridge University Press, 2005).

8 Amartya Sen, *Development as Freedom* (Anchor, 2000).

9 Kuznets, Baumol and Maddison in the USA, and Fourastié and Sauvy in France.

10 While productivity growth was situated around 2.8 per cent over the period 1959–73 and above 1.5 per cent during the period 1973–85, it then registered a rebound with an average rise of 2.6 per cent over the period 1985–2006.

11 Philippe Askenazy, 'La Croissance moderne', *Economica*, 2002.

12 Robert Gordon, *Macroeconomics*, 12th edn (Prentice-Hall, 2011).

13 The chronicle of the jump in tertiary productivity well illustrates the trend at work. Between 1987 and 2007, half of American productivity progress is explained by digitalization of society; a quarter by the computing sector itself; and a quarter by the use of new equipment. This period of euphoria culminated in the Internet bubble period that led to over-investment, particularly when fear of the Year 2000 bug induced firms to accelerate their programmes. Yet after 2000, and despite the bursting of the Internet bubble, productivity continued to increase at a rapid pace. 'Cost-cutting' was in full swing, and was translated into a major drop in the number of working hours. This tendency continued after the financial crisis of 2008. For the first time in the history of modern recessions, productivity is rising despite the fall in activity, while historically it has always been the reverse.

14 It is habitual to confuse the question of growth and that of unemployment. Full employment is certainly easier to attain when growth is strong, but the two obey different logics. I tackled this question in *Nos temps modernes* (Flammarion, 1999).

15 France and the United States devote 21 per cent of total employment to education and health (the same figure in both countries).

16 Christian Baudelot and Robert Establet, *L'Élitisme républicain*, 'La République des idées' (Paris: Le Seuil, 2009).

17 Brigitte Dormont, 'Les Dépenses de santé, une évolution salutaire', Editions rue d'Ulm. Collection du CEPREMAP.

18 Richard Barbrook, *Imaginary Future: From Thinking Machines to the Global Village* (London: Pluto, 2007), p. 283.

19 Maya Beauvallet, 'Portrait des musiciens à l'heure du numérique', Editions rue d'Ulm, Collection du CEPREMAP, 2011.

20 The GDP (= Gross Domestic Product) measures wealth at its market value. Many modifications have been proposed to make it more pertinent: to introduce into its calculation the net losses linked to the use of free goods (notably the environment) or to calculate the dispersal of income and take into account the division of wealth. See the report by Stiglitz-Fitoussi-Sen to the Commission on the Measurement of Economic Performance and Social Progress (2009) on all these issues. The OECD has proposed an index that includes 'well-being', but that aspect still poses less the problem of how to measure it than how to use it.

21 Martin Ravaillon, 'Poor or Just Feeling Poor? On Subjective Data in Measuring Poverty', CEPREMAP Conference on 'Happiness in Poor Countries', www.cepremap.ens.fr
  'The more blatant forms of inequality and exploitation survive in the world by making allies of the deprived and exploited. The underdog bears the burden so well that he or she overlooks the burden itself. Discontent is replaced by acceptance . . . suffering and anger by cheerful endurance.'

22 The worldwide success of the Metropolitan Opera's 'Live in HD' transmissions – and of other classical performances in

high definition – suggests that there still exist audiences that can be reached in the digital age.

23 The perspective of freedom also sheds light on the issue of salaried work. As Alain Supiot shows, the 'work contract' is supposed to govern symmetrical engagements of two parties who are presumed equal, the employer and the employee. But in reality the contract subjects the employee to a duty of obedience and subordination to the employer. According to Supiot, syndicalism got workers out of this impasse. The labour union incarnates the employee's freedom, enabling him to speak as an equal with the employer, despite the 'contract' that binds them.

24 Marshall Sahlins, *Stone Age Economics*, 2nd edn (London: Routledge, 2003); see also André Orléan, *L'Empire de la valeur* (Paris: Le Seuil, 2011) for a brilliant analysis of this passage.

25 Laurence Fontaine, 'La Justice sociale selon Amartya Sen', *Esprit*, 368 (October 2010).

Conclusion

1 Albert Hirschman, *The Passions and the Interests* (Princeton University Press, 1977).

2 Jean-Pierre Dupuy, *L'Avenir de l'économie* (Paris: Flammarion, 2012).

Index

Acemoglu, Daron 73–4
adaptation 9, 125
Adrianople, Battle of (378)
    38
advice, ten pieces of 18–19
age
    and happiness 10, 18
    agricultural employment 84
airline companies 21
Alcoholics Anonymous 50
altruism 19, 97
Ameisen, Jean-Claude 4, 96
American Eugenics Society 96
anomie 66
anonymity 93–4
anthropogenic growth 104,
    115
anti-depressants, consumption
    of 1
Arab countries 71
Arab Spring 71
Arendt, Hannah 93, 107
Aristide, Aelius 36, 37
Aristotle 13, 40, 100

Asia 60–2
    economic growth 61–2
Askenazy, Philippe 114
Athens 43
Atlan, Monique 101–2
Augustine, Saint 41
Augustulus, Romulus 38
Aurelius, Marcus 34
austerity measures 80–1, 82
Austria 79
autonomy 11

baby-boomers 4, 45, 46, 49,
    50
Baidu 63–4
Banerjee, Abijit 58, 59, 122
Barbero, Alessandro 38
Barbrook, Richard 118
Beauvallet, Maya 25, 27, 118
    Absurd Strategies 3
Becker, Gary 3
    A Treatise on the Family 12
Beethoven 10
Bell, Daniel 46, 113

Bell, Graham 92
Ben Ali 72
Bénabou, Roland 25–6, 94–5
Bentham, Jeremy 12
Bhutan 5
Big Blue computer 103, 104
bird flu 88
Blade Runner 103
blood donors 2–3, 24–5
Bo Xilai 69
Boeing 52
bonding capital 48
bonuses 2, 3, 27–8
Botswana
    and democracy 70–1
Bourdieu, Pierre 15
bourgeoisie 33
Boyer, Robert 104, 115
brain 6
Brazil 60
Bretton Woods conference
    (1944) 80
bridging capital 48
Britain 74
Brown, Peter 34, 35, 39
Brüning, Chancellor 81
Bundesbank 82
Bush, George W. 43, 52

Cannes summit (2011) 78
capability 121
capitalism 20, 22, 29, 118, 119
    4.0 70
    and democracy 68–72
    managerial 28
    new spirit of 24–8
Carrell, Alexis 96
Casilli, Antonio 92, 93
Castel, Robert 95
catastrophes, natural and
    human 87

Chalmin, Philippe 87
child mortality 58
chimpanzees 98, 100
China 60, 62–8, 73
    and American debt 78
    corruption scandals 69
    democracy and capitalism
        68–70
    economic growth 63, 65,
        68, 124
    and happiness 65, 66
    inequalities 64, 65, 77
    and Internet 63–4
    mercantilist doctrine 77
    pollution 64
    poor in 64, 65
    population 63
    and savings 77
    single child policy and
        deficit of girls 67–8
    surpassing of by West 56
    Tiananmen Square 68,
        124
    urban and rural happiness
        compared 66
    and world wealth 55
China Mobile 64
Chinese, ancient 50–1
Christianity
    and Roman Empire 38–41,
        126
civic spirit
    decline of in United States
        46–50
clash of civilizations 56
climatic disturbances 87
cloning 102
Cold War 29–30, 54
commodity fetishism 23
Communism 111
    digital 118

Community of Coal and Steel 83
company directors' pay 31–2
comparing oneself with others 7–8, 18, 19, 125
compensatory passion, theory of 124–5
competition 11–12, 125
and cooperation 26–7, 97, 125
matrimonial 12
complexity 89
computers 103–4
Comte-Sponville, Andre *Is Capitalism Moral?* 13–14, 22, 24
Condorcet Paradox 16–17
conglomerates 21
Constantine, Emperor 34, 38, 39
cooperation
and competition 26–7, 97, 125
corruption 72
cost-cutting, and economic growth 114–15
counter-gift 24
Cuba 73–4
Cultural Revolution 69
cybersex 94

DARPA (Defence Advanced Research Projects Agency) 52
Darwin, Charles 3–4, 95–7
The Genealogy of Man 97
The Origin of Species 96
Dawkins, Richard
The Selfish Gene 98–9
de Gaulle, General 60
de Waal, Frans 99

de-industrialization 83–6
Debord, Guy 107
Defence Advanced Research Projects Agency (DARPA) 52
Defence Department (US) 51–2, 103
Defoe, Daniel
Robinson Crusoe 15
democracy 68–75, 107
and Botswana 70–1
and capitalism 68–72
and China 68–70
and economic development/ growth 72–4, 75, 83
and education 73
and India 70, 74–5
Popper's definition 72
demographics 57
depression 1
desire 12–13
Detroit Treaty 28
diarrhoea
as major cause of child mortality 58
digital communism 118
digital economy 117–18, 125
digital revolution 114, 115
digital world 92–3
Diocletian, Emperor 38
disinterestedness 94–5
divorce 10–12
Diwan, Ishac 71, 72
DNA 103
Dormont, Brigitte 116
Draghi, Mario 82
Droit, Roger-Pol 101–2
Duflo, Esther 58, 59, 122
Dumont, Louis 40, 41
Dupas, Pascaline 59–60

Dupuy, Jean-Pierre 124
Durkheim, Emile 66

Easterlin, Richard 109, 112
Eastern Europe 66
Eaton, J. 86
economic growth 112
  and Asia 61–2
  and China 63, 65, 68, 124
  and cost-cutting 114–15
  and democracy 72–4, 75,
    83
  neo-Stakhanovist nature of
    114, 115
economic liberalism 77
economic revolution
  and anthropogenic
    revolution 104, 115
education 116
  and democracy 73
ego 11, 40, 41
Egypt 72
Ehrenberg, Alain 11
Eliot, T. S. 49
Elster, Jon 14
emerging countries 56, 60,
  78–9
  enrichment of poses
    problems for Western
    world 62, 87
  growth of 55, 57
  transition of 57
empathy 99
employment
  agricultural 84
  evolution in towards health
    and education 115–16
  industrial 83–4
'end of history' 107
Engels, Friedrich 111
Epicurus 12

epidemics 87–8
Etilé, Fabrice 7
eudaimonia (good life) 12–13
eugenics 96
euro 79, 80–1, 82, 83
euro zone 79
Europe 76
  distinction from United
    States 43–4
  in distress 79–83
  and financial crisis 79
  industrial employment 83
  industrial productivity
    84–5
European Central Bank 81–2
evergetism 43
exceptionalism
  and United States 50–3
extrinsic goods 8

Facebook 92, 117
farmer suicides (India) 57
Federal Reserve 81
Ferguson, Niall 43
financial crises 88–9
financial crisis (current) 78
  comparison with 1929 crisis
    78
  and Europe 81–2
  and globalization 83
  origins 76–7
financial rewards
  and moral rewards 2, 25
Finland
  and education 116
Fitzgerald, F. Scott 33
Fontaine, Laurence 122
Fordism 28
France 1, 76, 79, 81
  health expenditure 116
  industrial employment 83

and managerial
 capitalism 28
share of household expendi-
 ture devoted to food and
 leisure 109
surveyonlivingconditions
 110
Frank, Robert 32–3
Frey, Bruno 8, 10, 18
 Ten Pieces of Advice 18–19
Friedman, Milton 22
 A *Monetary History of the*
 United States 81
Fukuyama, Francis 107

Galton, Francis 96
GDP 120
General Electric 22
General Motors 28, 29
Generation X 46
genes 98–101
genetic body 101–5
genome sequencing 103
Germany 56, 73, 79
 industrial employment 85
 Nazi 81, 96
Gibbon, Edward 39
gift economy 118
gift/counter-gift 24
Glaeser, Edward 45, 73
globalization 53, 75, 76–9, 83,
 86, 87, 89
 and financial crisis 83
 as a hybrid process 91
 and unemployment 84
Godechot, Olivier 31
Gold Standard 79
good life 12–13
Google 63
Gordon, Robert 114–15
Goths 38

Great Compression 29
Great Depression 78
Greece, modern 79, 81
Greeks, ancient 40
Greenpeace 50
gross domestic happiness
 5–19
Gu Kailai 69

H1N1 virus 88
Habakkuk, H. J. 51
happiness 1, 10, 119–23
 and age 10, 18
 as an objective
 indicator 120
 and China 65, 66
 criticism of economic
 approach by Sen 121
 regression of in rich countries
 1
 secrets of 18
Haussmann, Ricardo 60
health expenditure 116–17
Held, Virginia 46
Henderson, Virginia 109
Hirschman, Albert 124
Hobbes, Thomas 1
Homo Numericus 91–4
Homo Politicus 72–5
Hong Kong 62
household expenditure 109
housing 110
Hu Yua 64
Huilin, Lu 64
humanists 104–5
Huntington, Samuel 56
hyper-class 31–3

IMF 78–9
incest, ban on 26–7
indebtedness 76–7

India 60, 61
  and democracy 70, 74–5
  elections (1991) 71
  farmer suicides 57
  life expectancy 61
  poverty in 57
individual/individualism 40–1
  and Roman Empire 40–1
  and United States 46, 49–50
Indonesia 61
industrial employment 83–4, 85
industrial mercantilism 85
industrial productivity 84–5
Industrial Revolution 55
inequalities 28–31
  and China 64, 65, 77
infectious diseases 87–8
influenza-A 87, 88
infotainment 49
Inglehart, Ronald 111–12
innovation, United States and
  quest for 51–2
INSEE 110
Institute of International
  Education 53
Internet 91–4, 117
  and China 63–4
  and solitude 94
'Internet and Life Satisfaction,
  The' study 94
intrinsic goods 8, 10
Ireland 81
Islamism, radical 71–2
Italy 81
Izraelewicz, Erik 62–3

Japan 60, 61–2
  2 Channel site 93–4
  economic growth 61–2
  industrial employment 85
job loss 10–11, 20, 84

Kahneman, Daniel 8
Kaletsky, Anatole 70
Kant, Immanuel 10
Kasparov, Gary 103, 104
Kennedy, John F. 46
Keynes, J. M. 80, 111
Khomeini, Ayatollah 74
Kindleberger, Charles 78
Knight, John 66
Kortum, S. 86
Krugman, Paul
  The Conscience of a Liberal
  29, 32
Kundera, Milan
  Testaments Betrayed 10
Kurzweil, Ray
  The Singularity is Near
  101–2

La Rochefoucauld 94
Landes, David 56
Late Antiquity 34–6, 37
Late-Modern World 106–8
Lawrence of Arabia (film)
  78
Layard, Richard 13
Lee Kwan Yew 70
left
  conflicts between right and
  107–8
Levi-Strauss, Claude 26–7
Levinas, Emmanuel 99
Lewis, Bernard
  What Went Wrong 71
liberalism 77
Limitless (film) 103–4
logic 15
lost time 8–9
Lyotard, Jean-François
  The Postmodern Condition
  106–7, 108, 113

machines
  people's relationship with
    103
  in Roman Empire 51
  and United States 51
malaria 58
Malaysia 61
Malthus, Thomas 95, 97
management by stress 22–4
management methods 21–2
managerial capitalism 28
Mandela, Nelson 71
Mao Zedong 66, 69
marriage 3, 12
Marx, Karl 23, 111, 115, 118, 119
Maslow, Alfred 109
matrimonial competition 12
Melitz, Marc 86
mercantilism, Chinese 77–8
middle class 29, 57
Mill, John Stuart 110–11
millionaires 9
Minnesota Twins Registry 98
mobile phones 112
modernity 54, 106, 107, 108
modernization 60
monetary rewards 25–6
Monopoly 33
moral rewards
  and financial reward 2, 25
moral/morality 2, 14, 22, 24, 25
Morgan, John Pierpont 31–2
Morishima 61–2
Mubarak 72
Muchenbled, Robert
  A History of Violence 67
Mumford, Lewis 56
Murdoch, Rupert 5

Murphy, Cullen 29
  Are We Rome? 42
musicians 118
Myrdal, Gunnar 61

natural selection 96
Nazism 81, 96
Neanderthal 99
needs 109
  Maslow's hierarchy of 109
neo-futurism 102
'new Cambridge
  Controversy' 72–3
New York 54
news, lowering of interest
  in 49
Nye, Joseph 42

Obama, Barack 45
Odyssey 14
old age 10
outsourcing 20–1

paganism 39–40
pandemics 87–8
parent-teacher associations
  (PTAs) (United States) 47
parity model 35, 39, 41
participatory surveillance 93
Pascal, Blaise 14
Pay without Performance 32
peak/end model 8
Pech, Thierry 33
Philippon, Thomas 31
Piketty, Thomas 31, 32
Pisani-Ferry, Jean 79
plague 88
Plato
  The Gorgias 12–13
Pollution
  in China 64

poor *see* poverty
Popper, Karl 72
population theory 95
Portugal 81
postindustrial economy 119
postindustrial society 4, 113, 115
postmaterialist society 108–12, 120
postmodernism 106–23
poverty 57–60, 112, 122
  in China 64, 65
  in India 57
  needing of institutional support for the poor 59
  progressive theory of 58–9
  Victorian theory of 58
prisons, privatization of 28
private property 43
Pro-Life movement 50
productivity 84, 86, 113–14
  digital 114
  growth of US 115
  industrial 84–5
  tertiary 113–14
Proudhon 119
Proust, Marcel
  In Search of Lost Time 8–9
psychoanalysis 6, 19
public sector 116
purpose of life 13
Putnam, Robert 5–6, 46–7, 48, 91–2
  Bowling Alone 46–7

Rabelais 10
radical Islamism 71–2
rankings, mania for 3
Rao, P. V. Narasimha 71

rationality 15–16
  and Condorcet Paradox 16–17
raw materials, rise in prices 87, 125
Reagan, Ronald 29
reciprocity 24, 97, 99, 125
religion
  and United States 48
  see also Christianity
representative democracy 107
research 116
residual inequalities 30
revolt (May 1968) 50
rewards
  financial and moral 2, 25
  offering monetary, to encourage children to work hard 25–6
Ricardo, David 60, 85
rich countries
  regression of happiness in 1
right
  conflicts between left and 107–8
rivalry 7
  and the workplace 22
Rizzolatti, Giacomo 99
Robbins, Lionel 15
Robinson Crusoe 15
robots 103
Roman Empire 34–41, 50–1
  and Athens 43
  changing in nature between Aurelius and Constantine 34–5
  and Christianity 38–41, 126
  crisis in public finances 37–8

emergence of
  soldier-emperors 38
fall of Western
  Empire 36–8, 42
and new conception of the
  individual 40–1
parallels between United
  States and 42–4, 52
penetration of by
  Barbarians 38
Romer, Paul 51
Rosedale, Philip 93
Rostow, Walt 56
Russia 74

Saez, Emmanuel 31, 32
Sahlins, Marshall 122
salaries 18
SARS virus 88
Saudi Arabia 71
savings
  and China 77
Schiavone, Aldo 36, 105
  Historie et destin 54
Schopenhauer, Arthur 8
scientific research 116
Second Life (video game) 93,
  119
Second World War 78
self-help groups 50
self-realization 109, 112
selfish gene 98–101
Sen, Amartya 67, 112, 120–2
  *Development as
  Freedom* 70
Senik, Claudia 7
September 11th (2001) 72
Servant, The (film) 77
service sector 113
Shanghai 54, 63
Simone, Rafaële 107–8

Singapore 61, 62, 70, 73
single-parent families 30–1
Singly, François de 10–11
slavery 44–5, 122
Smil, Vaclav 51
Smith, Adam
  *Theory of Moral
  Sentiments* 97
social capital 48
Social Network (film) 92
society, growing stratification
  of 30
solitude
  and Internet 94
South Korea 62, 73
Soviet Union, dissolution
  of 71
Spain 81
Spanish flu (1918–19) 88
Stark, Jurgen 82
Stein, Gertrude 54
stem cells 102
struggle for existence 3, 96, 97
sub-prime crisis 88–9
suicide 1
Swissre 87
sympathy 97

Taiwan 56, 62
Tang Fuzhen 70
Tea Party 45
telephone 92
television 5–7, 91, 112
  as an unsatisfying
    experience 6
  and baby-boomers 49
  and decline of American
    civil spirit 5–6
  impact of lifting ban on
    owning a set in Bhutan 5
  impact of on our lives 6–7

tertiary work 113–14
Third Industrial
    Revolution 114
three powers, theory of 14
Tiananmen Square 68, 124
'time inconsistency of
    preferences' 6
Tirole, Jean 25–6, 94–5
Tocqueville, Alexis de 11, 44,
    46, 51
Touraine, Alain 113
trade, international 86
trade unions
    and United States 47
trans-human world 101
transitivity 16
transport expenses 110
Triffin, Robert 80
Trust Game 23, 97
Tunisia 72
Turing, Alan 103
twins study 98
20001: A Space Odyssey 103

Ulysses and the Sirens 14
unemployment 84 *see also* job
    loss
United Auto Workers
    (UAW) 28
United States 1, 11, 29, 76
    anti-government stance
        44
    bird flu 88
    China and debt of 78
    decline of civic spirit 46–50
    decline in labour movement
        47–9
    economic failure (2008) 17
    evergetism 43
    and exceptionalism 50–3
    financial crisis (1930s) 81

foreign students at
    universities in 52–3
health expenditure 116
income disparities 76–7
and individualism 46,
    49–50
industrial employment 83
industrial productivity 84–5
inequalities 29–30
parallels with Roman
    Empire
    42–4, 52
private prisons 28
productivity growth 115
as promised land of Homo
    Economicus 44
PTAs 47
quest for innovation 51–2
and religion 48
slavery legacy 44–5
and television 5
voting in presidential
    elections 47
US Department of Defense
    51–2, 103

Valens, Emperor 38
Vernant, Jean-Pierre 40, 93
Veyne, Paul 39–40
virtual communities 91–2
virtual currencies 119
Vodafone 64

Wall Street Journal 72
Walmart 29
wealth
    desire for 124
    distribution of world 55
Weber, Axel 82
Weber, Henri 50
Weber, Max 27, 121

Weimar Republic 72, 74
Welch, Jack 22
West 56, 59
Williamson, Oliver 27
Wolff, Francis 100–1
work 20–33
    and job loss 10–11, 20, 84
    and management by stress
        22–4
    and moral behaviour 24
    and new spirit of capitalism
        24–8

rivalry in the workplace
    22
'working rich' 31–2
World Bank
    'The East Asian Miracle' 62
world growth 55

Yu Hua 65, 69, 124

Zakaria, Fareed 63
Zhang Xiaobo 67–8
Zuckerberg, Mark 92